Legal & Disclaimer

CONTENTS

TIPS ON USING AN AIR FRYING OVEN

Are you excited to bring variety to the table by using the air frying feature on your new Frigidaire appliance? Enjoy these helpful tips on how to get the most from your air fryer oven.

What foods can be cooked in an air fryer oven?

You can use the air fry setting on your oven for most foods that can traditionally be deep-fried. Some of our favorite recipes include:

- Chicken wings, chicken nuggets or pizza bites

- French fries, onion rings or sweet potato fries

- Brussel sprouts, kale, or zucchini fries

Can you cook battered food in an air fryer oven?

Crispy food needs enough oil to bind batters and coatings, but not too much or you'll end up with soggy results. If the food has a crumbly or floury outside texture, try spraying it with a little bit more oil.

If you're making air fried food from scratch, spray your homemade items with a light coating of oil (too much and the food won't get crispy) and arrange foods so the hot air circulates around each piece as much as possible.

Can you use olive oil while air frying?

Using cooking oils that can stand up to high temperatures is key while air frying, so avocado, grapeseed, and peanut oil are great for achieving crispy goodness. For best results, brush on lightly or spray an even coat of cooking spray made from these oils. Extra virgin olive oil is not an air fry-friendly oil due to its low smoke point, but extra light olive oil can be used for air frying because of its high smoke point. Other types of olive oil and some vegetable oils smoke at lower temperatures, meaning they will cause food to dry up quickly and prevent them from getting crispy.

Can you use aluminum foil in an air fryer oven?

Air fry works best on dark pans because they get and stay hot very quickly. Shiny foil reflects heat off the bakeware, which may change your results. When cooking with the Air fry Tray, we suggest putting a baking sheet on a rack a couple of positions below your tray. You can line that sheet with foil or parchment (or both) to catch any drips or crumbs, but you should never put aluminum foil, liners, or bakeware on the oven bottom. Items in this location can cause issues with air circulation and direct heat in any oven. Always keep the bottom of the oven clear so the air can circulate properly.

How do I keep my air frying oven clean?

Before using the air fry feature, place a cookie or baking sheet a rack or two under the Air Fry Tray to catch crumbs or drips. This will keep the bottom of the oven clean and free of fallen bits that can burn or cause odors later. Remember, do not place pans directly on the oven bottom to keep heat circulating correctly.

How do I clean the Air Fry Tray?

The Air Fry Tray is dishwasher safe, but for optimal cleaning, we recommend washing it by hand. It's designed to hold foods that already have some oil on them, which should keep food from sticking.

How do I limit the amount of smoke when using the Air Fry Tray?

Air fry uses really hot air to cook food fast and make it crunchy. Although air fry uses hot air to cook, remember that you are still frying your food so that it gets crispy! When some high-fat or greasy foods (like fresh wings) meet that hot air inside an oven, some smoke is normal. **If air fry is making a lot of smoke, try these tips:**

- When using the Air Fry Tray, put a baking sheet on a rack or two below the Air Fry Tray. This keeps drips and crumbs from landing on the oven bottom, where they can burn and create smoke. For additional protection, place some foil-lined parchment paper on the baking sheet. Parchment paper traps oil and keeps it from smoking.

- Use cooking oils that can stand up to high temperatures like avocado, grapeseed, and peanut oils. Cooking sprays made from these oils are available at the grocery store.

- Keep foil, parchment paper, and bakeware off the bottom of the oven. The oven bottom needs to stay clear so air can circulate.

- Don't overcrowd the food on your baking sheet or on the Air Fry Tray. If air can't circulate around each item, the cooking and crisping process may slow down and allow more grease to settle or drip.

- If your catch-tray is smoking, try placing parchment paper on it to hold grease. For extra-moist foods, you may have to use more. It's worth it!

- Some foods, like fresh wings and some vegetables, have a lot of moisture and may drip more than you expect. For items that might drip, use a pan with low sides if you're not using an Air Fry Tray.

- Air fry uses super-heated air, so if your oven bottom already has drips or crumbs on it (it happens!), those can smoke. Keep your oven bottom clean.

- If you have an oven vent, use it when cooking with air fry, like you would when using the cooktop.

BREAKFAST

Sunny-side Up Eggs

Servings: 2
Cooking Time: 3 Minutes

Ingredients:
- 2 large eggs
- Salt and freshly ground black pepper

Directions:
1. Crack the eggs into an oiled or nonstick small 4 × 8 × 2¼-inch loaf pan. Sprinkle with salt and pepper to taste.
2. TOAST once, or until the eggs are done to your preference.

Spicy Beef Fajitas

Servings: 4
Cooking Time: 40 Minutes

Ingredients:
- Mixture:
- 1 pound flank steak, cut into thin strips
- 2 inches long
- 1 bell pepper, seeded and cut into thin strips
- 2 tablespoons chopped onion
- 1 tablespoon chopped fresh cilantro
- ¼ teaspoon hot sauce
- 1 teaspoon garlic powder
- ½ teaspoon cumin
- 1 teaspoon chili powder
- Salt and freshly ground black pepper to taste
- 4 8-inch flour tortillas

Directions:
1. Combine all the mixture ingredients in an oiled or nonstick 8½ × 8½ × 2-inch square baking (cake) pan.
2. BROIL for 20 minutes, turning every 5 minutes, or until the pepper and onion are tender and the meat is beginning to brown. Remove from the oven and place equal portions of the mixture in the center of each tortilla. Roll the tortilla around the mixture and lay, seam side down, in a shallow baking pan.
3. BAKE at 350° F. for 20 minutes, or until the tortillas are lightly browned.

Cinnamon Toast

Servings: 2
Cooking Time: 2 Minutes

Ingredients:
- 1 tablespoon brown sugar
- 2 teaspoons margarine, at room temperature
- ¼ teaspoon ground cinnamon
- 2 slices whole wheat or multigrain bread

Directions:
1. Combine the sugar, margarine, and cinnamon in a small bowl with a fork until well blended. Spread each bread slice with equal portions of the mixture.
2. TOAST once, or until the sugar is melted and the bread is browned to your preference.

Good Stuff Bread

Servings: 2
Cooking Time: 40 Minutes

Ingredients:

- First mixture:
- 1 apple, peeled and grated
- 1 carrot, peeled and grated
- 1 cup unbleached flour
- 2 teaspoons baking powder
- ⅓ cup chopped walnuts
- ⅓ cup raisins
- ⅓ cup rolled oats
- ⅓ cup shredded sweetened coconut
- Blending mixture:
- 1 banana
- 1 egg
- 1 cup low-fat buttermilk
- 2 tablespoons dark brown sugar
- 2 tablespoons vegetable oil
- Salt to taste

Directions:

1. Preheat the toaster oven to 375° F.
2. Combine all the first mixture ingredients in a medium bowl and stir to mix well. Set aside.
3. Process all the blending mixture ingredients in a blender or food processor until the mixture is smooth. Add to the first mixture ingredients and stir to mix thoroughly. Transfer to an oiled or nonstick 8½ × 4½ × 2¼-inch regular size loaf pan.
4. BAKE for 40 minutes, or until a toothpick inserted in the center comes out clean and the top is well browned.

Avocado Chicken Flatbread

Servings: 4
Cooking Time: 9 Minutes

Ingredients:

- 1 tablespoon olive oil
- 1 clove garlic, minced
- 1 small avocado, pitted, peeled, and thinly sliced
- 1 teaspoon fresh lime juice
- ¼ cup ranch salad dressing
- 1 tablespoon Sriracha or hot sauce
- 1 package (10.6 ounces) flatbread pizza crust
- ¾ cup chopped, cooked chicken
- 2 slices bacon, cooked until crisp and crumbled
- ¼ cup chopped red onion
- ¾ cup shredded Monterey Jack cheese
- 1 cup thinly sliced romaine or iceberg lettuce
- ½ cup cherry tomatoes, halved

Directions:

1. Preheat the toaster oven to 400°F.
2. Mix the olive oil and garlic in a small bowl; set aside.
3. Place the avocado slices in a small bowl and drizzle with the lime juice; set aside.
4. Stir the salad dressing and Sriracha in a small bowl; set aside.
5. Brush the garlic olive oil over the flatbread. Place it on a 12-inch pan and bake for 3 to 4 minutes, or until the crust is hot and lightly toasted.
6. Top the crust with the chicken, bacon, onion, and cheese. Bake for 5 minutes or until the cheese is melted. Top with the lettuce, tomatoes, and avocado slices. Drizzle with the ranch dressing mixture.

Baked Curried Fruit

Servings: 4
Cooking Time: 25 Minutes

Ingredients:
- Curry mixture:
- 2 tablespoons dry white wine
- 1 teaspoon lemon juice
- ¼ teaspoon ground allspice
- ¼ teaspoon ground ginger
- ¼ teaspoon ground cardamom
- ¼ teaspoon turmeric
- ¼ teaspoon ground cumin
- ¼ teaspoon ground coriander
- Pinch of grated nutmeg
- Pinch of cayenne
- 2 tablespoons honey
- 1 teaspoon soy sauce
- 1 16-ounce can pear halves, drained
- 1 8-ounce can pineapple chunks, drained
- 1 16-ounce can peach halves

Directions:
1. Preheat the toaster oven to 350° F.
2. Combine the curry mixture ingredients in a 1-quart 8½ × 8½ × 4-inch ovenproof baking dish and add the fruit, mixing well.
3. BAKE, uncovered, for 25 minutes, or until bubbling and the sauce is thickened. Cool and serve on a sesame wafer with Creamy Yogurt Sauce.

Western Omelet

Servings: 2
Cooking Time: 22 Minutes

Ingredients:
- ¼ cup chopped onion
- ¼ cup chopped bell pepper, green or red
- ¼ cup diced ham
- 1 teaspoon butter
- 4 large eggs
- 2 tablespoons milk
- ⅛ teaspoon salt
- ¾ cup grated sharp Cheddar cheese

Directions:
1. Place onion, bell pepper, ham, and butter in air fryer oven baking pan. Air-fry at 390°F for 1 minute and stir. Continue cooking 5 minutes, until vegetables are tender.
2. Beat together eggs, milk, and salt. Pour over vegetables and ham in baking pan. Air-fry at 360°F for 15 minutes or until eggs set and top has browned slightly.
3. Sprinkle grated cheese on top of omelet. Cook 1 minute or just long enough to melt the cheese.

Paleo Spiced Zucchini Bread

Servings: 8

Cooking Time: 45 Minutes

Ingredients:
- Dry Ingredients
- 1½ cups almond flour
- 2 tablespoons coconut flour
- 1 teaspoon cinnamon
- ¼ teaspoon allspice
- ⅛ teaspoon ground cloves
- 1 teaspoon baking powder
- ½ teaspoon baking soda
- ¼ teaspoon salt
- 1 cup chopped walnuts
- Wet Ingredients
- ⅓ cup coconut sugar
- 1 teaspoon vanilla extract
- 3 large eggs
- 5 tablespoons olive oil
- 2 tablespoons applesauce
- 1 cup shredded zucchini, squeezed to remove excess moisture

Directions:
1. Stir together all the dry ingredients in a large bowl.
2. Whisk all the wet ingredients in a separate bowl.
3. Add the dry ingredients to the wet ingredients and stir to combine. Allow the batter to rest for 5 minutes. This allows the coconut flour to absorb the batter.
4. Preheat the toaster Oven to 350°F.
5. Grease the mini loaf pans with coconut oil spray. Divide the batter evenly between the pans.
6. Place the mini loaf pans on the wire rack, then insert the rack at mid position in the preheated oven.
7. Select the Bake function, adjust time to 45 minutes, and press Start/Pause.
8. Remove when a toothpick or cake tester inserted into the middle comes out clean.
9. Remove zucchini bread from the pans and place on a cooling rack for 15 minutes before slicing.

Huevos Rancheros

Servings: 2
Cooking Time: 60 Minutes

Ingredients:

- 1 (28-ounce) can diced tomatoes
- 1½ teaspoons packed brown sugar
- 1½ teaspoons lime juice
- 1 small onion, chopped
- ¼ cup canned chopped green chiles
- 2 tablespoons extra-virgin olive oil
- 1½ tablespoons chili powder
- 2 garlic cloves, sliced thin
- ¼ teaspoon plus ⅛ teaspoon table salt, divided
- 2 ounces pepper Jack cheese, shredded (½ cup)
- 4 large eggs
- ⅛ teaspoon pepper
- ½ avocado, halved, pitted, and diced
- 2 tablespoons minced fresh cilantro
- 2 scallions, sliced thin
- 4 (6-inch) corn tortillas, warmed

Directions:

1. Adjust toaster oven rack to middle position and preheat the toaster oven to 450 degrees. Drain tomatoes in fine-mesh strainer set over bowl, pressing with rubber spatula to extract as much juice as possible. Combine ¾ cup drained tomato juice, sugar, and lime juice in bowl; set aside. Discard remaining drained juice.
2. Combine tomatoes, onion, chiles, oil, chili powder, garlic, and ¼ teaspoon salt in bowl, then spread mixture evenly on small rimmed baking sheet. Roast until charred in spots, 25 to 30 minutes, stirring and redistributing mixture into even layer halfway through roasting.
3. Remove sheet from oven. Carefully stir reserved tomato juice mixture into roasted vegetables, season with salt and pepper to taste, and spread into even layer. Sprinkle pepper Jack over top and, using back of spoon, make 4 evenly spaced indentations in cheese, each about 3 inches in diameter. Crack 1 egg into each hole and sprinkle with remaining ⅛ teaspoon salt and pepper.
4. Roast until whites are just beginning to set but still have some movement when sheet is shaken, 7 to 8 minutes for runny yolks or 9 to 10 minutes for soft but set yolks. Top with avocado, cilantro, and scallions. Serve immediately with tortillas.

Bacon Cheddar Biscuits

Servings: 6
Cooking Time: 15 Minutes

Ingredients:
- 1 cup all-purpose flour
- 1 tablespoon baking powder
- ¼ teaspoon table salt
- ¼ teaspoon smoked paprika or freshly ground black pepper
- 3 tablespoons unsalted butter
- ½ cup whole milk
- 1 cup shredded sharp cheddar cheese
- 2 tablespoons minced fresh chives
- 4 slices bacon, cooked until crisp and crumbled

Directions:
1. Preheat the toaster oven to 425°F.
2. Stir the flour, baking powder, salt, and paprika in a large bowl. Using a pastry cutter or two knives, cut the butter into the flour mixture until the mixture is crumbly throughout. Pour in the milk and gently mix until just combined. Stir in the cheese, chives, and bacon.
3. Turn the dough onto a lightly floured surface and knead lightly about 8 times. Roll the dough, using a rolling pin, until about ¾ inch thick. Cut out rounds using a 2-inch cutter. Place 1 inch apart on an ungreased 12 x 12-inch baking pan. Bake for 12 to 15 minutes or until golden brown.

Baked Steel-cut Oatmeal

Servings: 2
Cooking Time: 60 Minutes

Ingredients:

- ½ cup steel-cut oats
- 1 tablespoon unsalted butter, cut into 2 pieces
- 2 cups boiling water, plus extra as needed
- ⅛ teaspoon table salt

Directions:

1. Adjust toaster oven rack to middle position and preheat the toaster oven to 450 degrees. Place oats and butter in 8-inch square baking dish or pan and bake until oats are golden brown and fragrant, 5 to 7 minutes, stirring thoroughly halfway through baking to incorporate butter into oats.

2. Remove pan from oven and reduce oven temperature to 325 degrees. Carefully stir boiling water and salt into oats and bake until oats are softened but still retain some chew and mixture thickens and resembles warm pudding, 40 to 45 minutes, rotating pan halfway through baking. Remove pan from oven, cover, and let sit for 5 minutes. Stir oatmeal to recombine and adjust consistency with extra boiling water as needed. Serve.

Buttermilk Biscuits

Servings: 6
Cooking Time: 15minutes

Ingredients:
- 2 cups unbleached flour
- 1 tablespoon baking powder
- ½ teaspoon baking soda
- Salt
- 3 tablespoons margarine, at room temperature
- 1 cup low-fat buttermilk
- Vegetable oil

Directions:
1. Preheat the toaster oven to 400° F.
2. Combine the flour, baking powder, baking soda, and salt to taste in a medium bowl.
3. Cut in the margarine with 2 knives or a pastry blender until the mixture is crumbly.
4. Stir in the buttermilk, adding just enough so the dough will stay together when pinched.
5. KNEAD the dough on a floured surface for one minute, then pat or roll out the dough to ¾ inch thick. Cut out biscuit rounds with a 2½-inch biscuit cutter. Place the rounds on an oiled or nonstick 6½ × 10inch baking sheet.
6. BAKE for 15 minutes, or until golden brown.

LUNCH AND DINNER

Slow Cooker Chicken Philly Cheesesteak Sandwich

Servings: 4
Cooking Time: 2 Minutes

Ingredients:
- 1 3/4 to 2 pounds chicken tenders
- 2 large green peppers, cut in strips
- 2 medium onions, sliced
- 1 1/2 tablespoons rotisserie seasoning
- 1/2 teaspoon salt
- 4 tablespoons Italian salad dressing
- 4 hoagie rolls, split
- 4 slices Cheddar or American cheese
- 1/4 cup banana pepper rings, optional
- Hot Sauce or ketchup, optional

Directions:
1. In slow cooker crock, combine chicken tenders, pepper strips and onion slices with rotisserie seasoning and salt.
2. Cook on HIGH for 2 to 2 1/2 hours or LOW for 4 to 5 hours.
3. Preheat the toaster oven broiler. Open rolls and place on a cookie sheet
4. Slice chicken tenders. Place back in slow cooker. With a slotted spoon, divide chicken, peppers and onions among rolls and drizzle with Italian dressing. Top with cheese slices.
5. Place under broiler until cheese is melted, about 2 minutes.
6. Serve with banana peppers, hot sauce or ketchup, if desired.

Oven-baked Barley

Servings: 2
Cooking Time: 60 Minutes

Ingredients:
- ⅓ cup barley, toasted
- Seasonings:
- 1 tablespoon sesame oil
- 1 tablespoon sesame seeds
- ¼ teaspoon ground cumin
- ¼ teaspoon turmeric
- ½ teaspoon garlic powder
- Salt and freshly ground black pepper to taste

Directions:
1. Combine the barley and 1½ cups water in a 1-quart 8½ × 8½ × 4-inch ovenproof baking dish. Cover with aluminum foil.
2. BAKE, covered, for 50 minutes, or until almost cooked, testing the grains after 30 minutes for softness.
3. Add the oil and seasonings and fluff with a fork to combine. Cover and let the barley sit for 10 minutes to finish cooking and absorb the flavors of the seasonings. Fluff once more before serving.

Oven-baked Couscous

Servings: 4
Cooking Time: 10 Minutes

Ingredients:

- 1 10-ounce package couscous
- 2 tablespoons olive oil
- 2 tablespoons canned chickpeas
- 2 tablespoons canned or frozen green peas
- 1 tablespoon chopped fresh parsley
- 3 scallions, chopped
- Salt and pepper to taste

Directions:

1. Preheat the toaster oven to 400° F.
2. Mix together all the ingredients with 2 cups water in a 1-quart 8½ × 8½ × 4-inch ovenproof baking dish. Adjust the seasonings to taste. Cover with aluminum foil.
3. BAKE, covered, for 10 minutes, or until the couscous and vegetables are tender. Adjust the seasonings to taste and fluff with a fork before serving.

Quick Pan Pizza

Servings: 8

Cooking Time: 22 Minutes

Ingredients:

- 1 can (13.8 oz.) refrigerator pizza crust, cut in half
- 2 tablespoons oil, divided
- 2/3 cup Slow Cooker Marinara Sauce, divided
- 2 cups shredded mozzarella cheese, divided
- 18 slices pepperoni, divided
- 1 small green pepper, sliced into rings, divided
- 2 large mushrooms, sliced, divided

Directions:

1. Preheat the toaster oven to 425°F. Spray baking pan with nonstick cooking spray.
2. Press half of dough into pan. Brush with 1 tablespoon oil.
3. Bake 8 to 9 minutes or until light brown.
4. Top baked crust with 1/3 cup sauce, 1 cup shredded mozzarella cheese and half of the pepperoni, green pepper and mushrooms.
5. Bake an additional 11 to 13 minutes or until cheese is melted and crust is brown. Repeat to make second pizza.

Individual Baked Eggplant Parmesan

Servings: 5
Cooking Time: 55 Minutes

Ingredients:

- 1 medium eggplant, cut into 1/2-inch thick slices
- 1 1/2 teaspoons salt
- 1 cup Slow Cooker Marinara Sauce
- 1 package (8 oz.) fresh mozzarella, cut into 8 slices, divided
- 1 package (0.75 oz.) fresh basil, leaves only, divided
- 1/4 cup grated Parmesan cheese, divided

Directions:

1. Sprinkle eggplant with salt and place in a colander to drain for 1 hour.
2. Preheat the toaster oven to 375°F. Spray baking pan and 5 (4-inch) ramekins with nonstick cooking spray.
3. Rinse eggplant thoroughly with water to remove salt. Press each slice between paper towels to remove extra water and salt. Place on papertowels to dry. Arrange a single layer of eggplant slices in baking pan.
4. Bake 25 to 30 minutes or until eggplant is tender. Remove slices to cooking rack. Repeat baking remaining eggplant. Reduce oven temperature to 350°F.
5. In each ramekin, layer 1 slice eggplant, 1 tablespoon sauce, 1 slice mozzarella, 1 basil leaf, 1 additional tablespoon sauce and sprinkle with Parmesan cheese. Repeat layers ending with a sprinkle of Parmesan cheese.
6. Bake 20 to 25 minutes or until cheese is melted and eggplant layers are heated through.

Nice + Easy Baked Macaroni + Cheese

Servings: 6
Cooking Time: 35 Minutes

Ingredients:

- Nonstick cooking spray
- 2 cups whole milk
- 3 ounces cream cheese
- ½ teaspoon kosher salt
- 1 clove garlic
- ¼ teaspoon freshly ground black pepper
- 8 ounces macaroni, uncooked
- 2 cups shredded cheddar cheese
- 2 tablespoons unsalted butter, melted
- ¼ cup grated Parmesan cheese
- 1 cup panko bread crumbs

Directions:

1. Preheat the toaster oven to 425°F. Spray an 11 x 7 x 2 ½-inch baking dish with nonstick cooking spray.
2. Place the milk, cream cheese, salt, garlic, and pepper into a blender. Blend until smooth.
3. Add macaroni to the prepared dish. Sprinkle with the cheddar cheese. Pour the milk mixture over all.
4. Combine the butter, Parmesan, and panko in a small bowl. Sprinkle the crumb mixture over the macaroni. Bake, uncovered, for 25 to 35 minutes or until the top is golden brown. Remove from the oven and let stand for at least 10 minutes.

Pea Soup

Servings: 6
Cooking Time: 55 Minutes

Ingredients:

- 1 cup dried split peas, ground in a blender to a powderlike consistency
- 3 strips lean turkey bacon, uncooked and chopped
- ¼ cup grated carrots
- ¼ cup grated celery
- 2 tablespoons grated onion
- ½ teaspoon garlic powder
- Salt and freshly ground black pepper to taste
- Garnish:
- 2 tablespoons chopped fresh chives

Directions:

1. Preheat the toaster oven to 400° F.
2. Combine all the ingredients in a 1-quart 8½ × 8½ × 4-inch ovenproof baking dish, mixing well. Adjust the seasonings.
3. BAKE, covered, for 35 minutes. Remove from the oven and stir.
4. BAKE, covered, for another 20 minutes, or until the soup is thickened. Ladle the soup into individual soup bowls and garnish each with chopped fresh chives.

Rosemary Lentils

Servings: 2

Cooking Time: 35 Minutes

Ingredients:
- ¼ cup lentils
- 1 tablespoon mashed Roasted Garlic
- 1 rosemary sprig
- 1 bay leaf
- Salt and freshly ground black pepper
- 2 tablespoons low-fat buttermilk
- 2 tablespoons tomato sauce

Directions:
1. Preheat the toaster oven to 400° F.
2. Combine the lentils, 1¼ cups water, garlic, rosemary sprig, and bay leaf in a 1-quart 8½ × 8½ × 4-inch ovenproof baking dish, stirring to blend well. Add the salt and pepper to taste. Cover with aluminum foil.
3. BAKE, covered, for 35 minutes, or until the lentils are tender. Remove the rosemary sprig and bay leaf and stir in the buttermilk and tomato sauce. Serve immediately.

Healthy Southwest Stuffed Peppers

Servings: 6
Cooking Time: 30 Minutes

Ingredients:

- 1 tablespoon oil
- 1 small onion, chopped
- 1 garlic clove, minced
- 1/2 pound ground turkey
- 1/2 cup drained black beans
- 1/2 cup whole kernel corn
- 1 jar (16 oz.) medium salsa, divided
- 1/2 cup cooked white rice
- 1/2 teaspoon chili powder
- 1/2 teaspoon salt
- 1/4 teaspoon ground cumin
- 1/4 teaspoon black pepper
- 3 medium peppers, halved lengthwise leaving stem on, seeded
- 1/3 cup shredded Monterey Jack cheese, divided
- Sour cream
- Chopped fresh cilantro

Directions:

1. Preheat the toaster oven to 350°F. Spray baking pan with nonstick cooking spray.
2. In a large skillet over medium-high, heat oil. Add onion and garlic, cook for 2 to 3 minutes.
3. Add turkey to skillet, cook, stirring frequently, for 6 to 8 minutes or until turkey is cooked through.
4. Stir black beans, corn, 1/2 cup salsa, rice, chili powder, salt, cumin and pepper into turkey mixture.
5. Fill each pepper half with turkey mixture, dividing mixture evenly among peppers.
6. Top each pepper half with remaining salsa.
7. Bake 20 minutes. Sprinkle with cheese and bake an additional 10 minutes or until heated through.
8. Top with sour cream and cilantro.

Inspirational Personal Pizza

Servings: 1
Cooking Time: 30 Minutes

Ingredients:
- 1 9-inch ready-made pizza crust
- 1 teaspoon olive oil
- 2 tablespoons tomato paste
- 4 ounces (½ cup) ground lean turkey breast
- 2 tablespoons sliced marinated artichokes
- 2 tablespoons pitted and chopped kalamata olives
- 2 tablespoons crumbled feta cheese
- 1 tablespoon chopped fresh basil leaves
- 1 tablespoon chopped fresh oregano leaves
- 2 tablespoons grated Parmesan cheese
- ¼ teaspoon red pepper flakes

Directions:
1. Preheat the toaster oven to 375°F.
2. Brush the pizza crust with the olive oil and spread on the tomato paste. Add all the other ingredients. Place the pizza on the toaster oven rack.
3. BAKE for 30 minutes, or until the topping is cooked and the crust is lightly browned.

Individual Chicken Pot Pies

Servings: 4
Cooking Time: 25 Minutes

Ingredients:

- 3 tablespoons unsalted butter
- ½ medium onion, chopped
- 1 carrot, chopped
- 1 stalk celery, chopped
- 1 ¼ cups sliced button or white mushrooms
- 2 tablespoons all-purpose flour
- 1 ¼ cups whole milk
- 1 tablespoon fresh lemon juice
- ½ teaspoon dried thyme leaves
- Kosher salt and freshly ground black pepper
- 1 ½ cups chopped cooked chicken
- ½ cup frozen peas
- Nonstick cooking spray
- 1 sheet frozen puff pastry, about 9 inches square, thawed (½ of a 17.3-ounce package)
- 1 large egg

Directions:

1. Melt the butter in a large skillet over medium-high heat. Add the onion, carrot, and celery and cook, stirring frequently, for 3 minutes. Add the mushrooms and cook, stirring frequently, for 7 to 10 minutes or until the liquid has evaporated. Blend in the flour and cook, stirring for 1 minute. (Be sure all of the flour is blended into the butter and vegetables.) Gradually stir in the milk. Cook, stirring constantly, until the mixture bubbles and thickens. Stir in the lemon juice and thyme and season with salt and pepper. Stir in the chicken and peas. Remove from the heat and set aside.

2. Preheat the toaster oven to 375°F. Spray 4 (8-ounce) oven-safe ramekins with nonstick cooking spray.

3. Roll the puff pastry out on a lightly floured board, to make an even 10-inch square. Cut the pastry into circles using a 4-inch cutter.

4. Spoon a heaping ¾ cup of filling into each prepared ramekin. Place a puff pastry circle on top of each and crimp the edges to seal to the ramekin. Using the tip of a paring knife, cut 3 slits in each crust to allow steam to escape. Whisk the egg with 1 tablespoon water in a small bowl. Brush the egg mixture over the top of the crust.

5. Bake for 20 to 25 minutes, or until the crust is golden brown. Remove from the oven and let stand for 5 minutes before serving.

Parmesan Artichoke Pizza

Servings: 6
Cooking Time: 15 Minutes

Ingredients:
- CRUST
- ¾ cup warm water (110°F)
- 1 ½ teaspoons active dry yeast
- ¼ teaspoon sugar
- 1 tablespoon olive oil
- 1 teaspoon table salt
- ⅓ cup whole wheat flour
- 1 ½ to 1 ⅔ cups bread flour
- TOPPINGS
- 2 tablespoons olive oil
- 1 teaspoon Italian seasoning
- 1 clove garlic, minced
- ½ cup whole milk ricotta cheese, at room temperature
- ⅔ cup drained, chopped marinated artichokes
- ¼ cup chopped red onion
- 3 tablespoons minced fresh basil
- ½ cup shredded Parmesan cheese
- ⅓ cup shredded mozzarella cheese

Directions:

1. Make the Crust: Place the warm water, yeast, and sugar in a large mixing bowl for a stand mixer. Stir, then let stand for 3 to 5 minutes or until bubbly.

2. Stir in the olive oil, salt, whole wheat flour, and 1 ½ cups bread flour. If the dough is too sticky, stir in an additional 1 to 2 tablespoons bread flour. Beat with the flat (paddle) beater at medium-speed for 5 minutes (or knead by hand for 5 to 7 minutes or until the dough is smooth and elastic). Place in a greased large bowl, turn the dough over, cover with a clean towel, and let stand for 30 to 45 minutes, or until starting to rise.

3. Stir the olive oil, Italian seasoning, and garlic in a small bowl; set aside.

4. Preheat the toaster oven to 450°F. Place a 12-inch pizza pan in the toaster oven while it is preheating.

5. Turn the dough onto a lightly floured surface and pull or roll the dough to make a 12-inch circle. Carefully transfer the crust to the hot pan.

6. Brush the olive oil mixture over the crust. Spread the ricotta evenly over the crust. Top with the artichokes, red onions, fresh basil, Parmesan, and mozzarella. Bake for 13 to 15 minutes, or until the crust is golden brown and the cheese is melted. Let stand for 5 minutes before cutting.

FISH AND SEAFOOD

Flounder Fillets

Servings: 4
Cooking Time: 8 Minutes

Ingredients:
- 1 egg white
- 1 tablespoon water
- 1 cup panko breadcrumbs
- 2 tablespoons extra-light virgin olive oil
- 4 4-ounce flounder fillets
- salt and pepper
- oil for misting or cooking spray

Directions:
1. Preheat the toaster oven to 390°F.
2. Beat together egg white and water in shallow dish.
3. In another shallow dish, mix panko crumbs and oil until well combined and crumbly (best done by hand).
4. Season flounder fillets with salt and pepper to taste. Dip each fillet into egg mixture and then roll in panko crumbs, pressing in crumbs so that fish is nicely coated.
5. Spray air fryer oven with nonstick cooking spray and add fillets. Air-fry at 390°F for 3 minutes.
6. Spray fish fillets but do not turn. Cook 5 minutes longer or until golden brown and crispy. Using a spatula, carefully remove fish from air fryer oven and serve.

Beer-breaded Halibut Fish Tacos

Servings: 4

Cooking Time: 10 Minutes

Ingredients:

- 1 pound halibut, cut into 1-inch strips
- 1 cup light beer
- 1 jalapeño, minced and divided
- 1 clove garlic, minced
- ¼ teaspoon ground cumin
- ½ cup cornmeal
- ¼ cup all-purpose flour
- 1¼ teaspoons sea salt, divided
- 2 cups shredded cabbage
- 1 lime, juiced and divided
- ¼ cup Greek yogurt
- ¼ cup mayonnaise
- 1 cup grape tomatoes, quartered
- ½ cup chopped cilantro
- ¼ cup chopped onion
- 1 egg, whisked
- 8 corn tortillas

Directions:

1. In a shallow baking dish, place the fish, the beer, 1 teaspoon of the minced jalapeño, the garlic, and the cumin. Cover and refrigerate for 30 minutes.

2. Meanwhile, in a medium bowl, mix together the cornmeal, flour, and ½ teaspoon of the salt.

3. In large bowl, mix together the shredded cabbage, 1 tablespoon of the lime juice, the Greek yogurt, the mayonnaise, and ½ teaspoon of the salt.

4. In a small bowl, make the pico de gallo by mixing together the tomatoes, cilantro, onion, ¼ teaspoon of the salt, the remaining jalapeño, and the remaining lime juice.

5. Remove the fish from the refrigerator and discard the marinade. Dredge the fish in the whisked egg; then dredge the fish in the cornmeal flour mixture, until all pieces of fish have been breaded.

6. Preheat the toaster oven to 350°F.

7. Place the fish in the air fryer oven and spray liberally with cooking spray. Air-fry for 6 minutes, flip the fish, and cook another 4 minutes.

8. While the fish is cooking, heat the tortillas in a heavy skillet for 1 to 2 minutes over high heat.

9. To assemble the tacos, place the battered fish on the heated tortillas, and top with slaw and pico de gallo. Serve immediately.

Maple Balsamic Glazed Salmon

Servings: 4
Cooking Time: 10 Minutes

Ingredients:
- 4 (6-ounce) fillets of salmon
- salt and freshly ground black pepper
- vegetable oil
- ¼ cup pure maple syrup
- 3 tablespoons balsamic vinegar
- 1 teaspoon Dijon mustard

Directions:
1. Preheat the toaster oven to 400°F.
2. Season the salmon well with salt and freshly ground black pepper. Spray or brush the bottom of the air fryer oven with vegetable oil and place the salmon fillets inside. Air-fry the salmon for 5 minutes.
3. While the salmon is air-frying, combine the maple syrup, balsamic vinegar and Dijon mustard in a small saucepan over medium heat and stir to blend well. Let the mixture simmer while the fish is cooking. It should start to thicken slightly, but keep your eye on it so it doesn't burn.
4. Brush the glaze on the salmon fillets and air-fry for an additional 5 minutes. The salmon should feel firm to the touch when finished and the glaze should be nicely browned on top. Brush a little more glaze on top before removing and serving with rice and vegetables, or a nice green salad.

Garlic-lemon Shrimp Skewers

Servings: 2
Cooking Time: 8 Minutes

Ingredients:

- Juice and zest of 1 lemon
- 1 tablespoon olive oil
- ½ teaspoon garlic puree
- ¼ teaspoon smoked paprika
- 12 large shrimp, peeled and deveined
- Oil spray (hand-pumped)
- Sea salt, for seasoning
- Freshly ground black pepper, for seasoning
- 1 tablespoon chopped fresh parsley

Directions:

1. Preheat the toaster oven to 350°F on AIR FRY for 5 minutes.
2. In a medium bowl, stir the lemon juice, lemon zest, olive oil, garlic, and paprika.
3. Add the shrimp and toss to combine. Cover, refrigerate, and let marinate for 30 minutes.
4. Soak 4 wooden skewers in water while the shrimp marinate.
5. Place the air-fryer basket in the baking tray and spray it generously with the oil.
6. Thread 3 shrimp on each skewer and place them in the basket. Discard any remaining marinade.
7. In position 2, air fry for 8 minutes, turning halfway through, until just cooked.
8. Season with the salt and pepper and serve topped with the parsley.

Shrimp & Grits

Servings: 4
Cooking Time: 5 Minutes

Ingredients:

- 1 pound raw shelled shrimp, deveined (26–30 count or smaller)
- Marinade
- 2 tablespoons lemon juice
- 2 tablespoons Worcestershire sauce
- 1 tablespoon olive oil
- 1 teaspoon Old Bay Seasoning
- ½ teaspoon hot sauce
- Grits
- ¾ cup quick cooking grits (not instant)
- 3 cups water
- ½ teaspoon salt
- 1 tablespoon butter
- ½ cup chopped green bell pepper
- ½ cup chopped celery
- ½ cup chopped onion
- ½ teaspoon oregano
- ¼ teaspoon Old Bay Seasoning
- 2 ounces sharp Cheddar cheese, grated

Directions:

1. Stir together all marinade ingredients. Pour marinade over shrimp and set aside.
2. For grits, heat water and salt to boil in saucepan on stovetop. Stir in grits, lower heat to medium-low, and cook about 5 minutes or until thick and done.
3. Place butter, bell pepper, celery, and onion in air fryer oven baking pan. Air-fry at 390°F for 2 minutes and stir. Cook 6 or 7 minutes longer, until crisp tender.
4. Add oregano and 1 teaspoon Old Bay to cooked vegetables. Stir in grits and cheese and air-fry at 390°F for 1 minute. Stir and cook 1 to 2 minutes longer to melt cheese.
5. Remove baking pan from air fryer oven. Cover with plate to keep warm while shrimp cooks.
6. Drain marinade from shrimp. Place shrimp in air fryer oven and air-fry at 360°F for 3 minutes. Cook 2 more minutes, until done.
7. To serve, spoon grits onto plates and top with shrimp.

Romaine Wraps With Shrimp Filling

Servings: 4

Cooking Time: 8 Minutes

Ingredients:

- Filling:
- 1 6-ounce can tiny shrimp, drained, or 1 cup fresh shrimp, peeled, cooked, and chopped
- ¾ cup canned chickpeas, mashed into 1 tablespoon olive oil
- 2 tablespoons chopped fresh parsley
- 2 tablespoons grated carrot
- 2 tablespoons chopped bell pepper
- 2 tablespoons minced onion
- 2 tablespoons lemon juice
- 1 teaspoon soy sauce
- Freshly ground black pepper to taste
- 4 large romaine lettuce leaves Olive oil
- 3 tablespoons lemon juice
- 1 teaspoon paprika

Directions:

1. Combine the filling ingredients in a bowl, adjusting the seasonings to taste. Spoon equal portions of the filling into the centers of the romaine leaves. Fold the leaves in half, pressing the filling together, overlap the leaf edges, and skewer with toothpicks to fasten. Carefully place the leaves in an oiled or nonstick 8½ × 8½ × 2-inch square baking (cake) pan. Lightly spray or brush the lettuce rolls with olive oil.

2. BROIL for 8 minutes, or until the filling is cooked and the leaves are lightly browned. Remove from the oven, remove the toothpicks, and drizzle with the lemon juice and sprinkle with paprika.

Crispy Smelts

Servings: 3
Cooking Time: 20 Minutes

Ingredients:
- 1 pound Cleaned smelts
- 3 tablespoons Tapioca flour
- Vegetable oil spray
- To taste Coarse sea salt or kosher salt

Directions:
1. Preheat the toaster oven to 400°F.
2. Toss the smelts and tapioca flour in a large bowl until the little fish are evenly coated.
3. Lay the smelts out on a large cutting board. Lightly coat both sides of each fish with vegetable oil spray.
4. When the machine is at temperature, set the smelts close together in the air fryer oven, with a few even overlapping on top. Air-fry undisturbed for 20 minutes, until lightly browned and crisp.
5. Remove from the machine and turn out the fish onto a wire rack. The smelts will most likely come out as one large block, or maybe in a couple of large pieces. Cool for a minute or two, then sprinkle the smelts with salt and break the block(s) into much smaller sections or individual fish to serve.

Roasted Fish With Provençal Crumb Topping

Servings: 3

Cooking Time: 25 Minutes

Ingredients:

- 1 tablespoon olive oil, plus more for greasing
- ⅓ cup finely chopped onion
- 1 clove garlic, minced
- ¾ cup fresh bread crumbs
- 2 tablespoons chopped fresh flat-leaf (Italian) parsley
- 1 teaspoon fresh thyme leaves
- 3 (5-ounce) cod fillets, or other white-fleshed, mild-flavored fish, patted dry (about 1 ¼ inches thick)
- 2 tablespoons dry white wine
- 2 teaspoons fresh lemon juice

Directions:

1. Preheat the toaster oven to 400°F. Lightly grease the baking pan with olive oil.

2. Heat the tablespoon of olive oil in a small skillet over medium-high heat. Add the onion and cook, stirring frequently, for 3 to 4 minutes, or until tender. Add the garlic and cook for 30 seconds. Remove the skillet from the heat. Stir in the bread crumbs, parsley, and thyme.

3. Place the fish in the prepared pan. Drizzle with the wine. Divide the crumb mixture evenly over the top of each fish fillet, and press onto the fillets. Roast for 20 to 25 minutes, or until the top is brown and the fish is opaque and flakes easily when tested with a fork. Sprinkle the lemon juice evenly over the fish.

Sea Scallops

Servings: 4
Cooking Time: 8 Minutes

Ingredients:
- 1½ pounds sea scallops
- salt and pepper
- 2 eggs
- ½ cup flour
- ½ cup plain breadcrumbs
- oil for misting or cooking spray

Directions:
1. Rinse scallops and remove the tough side muscle. Sprinkle to taste with salt and pepper.
2. Beat eggs together in a shallow dish. Place flour in a second shallow dish and breadcrumbs in a third.
3. Preheat the toaster oven to 390°F.
4. Dip scallops in flour, then eggs, and then roll in breadcrumbs. Mist with oil or cooking spray.
5. Place scallops in air fryer oven in a single layer, leaving some space between. You should be able to cook about a dozen at a time.
6. Air-fry at 390°F for 8 minutes, watching carefully so as not to overcook. Scallops are done when they turn opaque all the way through. They will feel slightly firm when pressed with tines of a fork.
7. Repeat step 6 to cook remaining scallops.

Roasted Pepper Tilapia

Servings: 6

Cooking Time: 20 Minutes

Ingredients:

- 6 5-ounce tilapia fillets
- 2 tablespoons olive oil
- Filling:
- 1 cucumber, peeled, seeds scooped out and discarded, and chopped
- ½ cup chopped roasted peppers, drained
- 2 tablespoons lemon juice
- 2 tablespoons chopped fresh parsley or cilantro
- 1 teaspoon garlic powder
- 1 teaspoon paprika
- Salt and freshly ground black pepper to taste
- Dip mixture:
- 1 cup nonfat sour cream
- 2 tablespoons low-fat mayonnaise
- 3 tablespoons Dijon mustard
- 1 teaspoon Worcestershire sauce
- 1 teaspoon dried dill

Directions:

1. Combine the filling ingredients in a bowl, adjusting the seasonings to taste.
2. Spoon equal portions of filling in the centers of the tilapia filets. Roll up the fillets, starting at the smallest end. Secure each roll with toothpicks and place the rolls in an oiled or nonstick baking pan. Carefully brush the fillets with oil and place them in an oiled or nonstick 8½ × 8½ × 2-inch square baking (cake) pan.
3. BROIL for 20 minutes, or until the fillets are lightly browned. Combine the dip mixture ingredients in a small bowl and serve with the fish.

Pecan-topped Sole

Servings: 4
Cooking Time: 12 Minutes

Ingredients:

- 4 (4-ounce) sole fillets
- Sea salt, for seasoning
- Freshly ground black pepper, for seasoning
- 1 cup crushed pecans
- ½ cup seasoned bread crumbs
- 1 large egg
- 2 tablespoons water
- Oil spray (hand-pumped)

Directions:

1. Preheat the toaster oven to 375°F on BAKE for 5 minutes.
2. Line the baking tray with parchment paper.
3. Pat the fish dry with paper towels and lightly season with salt and pepper.
4. In a small bowl, stir the pecans and bread crumbs.
5. In another small bowl, beat the egg and water until well blended.
6. Dredge the fish in the egg mixture, shaking off any excess, then in the nut mixture.
7. Place the fish in the baking sheet and repeat with the remaining fish.
8. Lightly spray the fillets with the oil on both sides.
9. In position 2, bake until golden and crispy, turning halfway, for 12 minutes in total. Serve.

POULTRY

Fried Chicken

Servings: 4
Cooking Time: 40 Minutes

Ingredients:

- 12 skin-on chicken drumsticks
- 1 cup buttermilk
- 1½ cups all-purpose flour
- 1 tablespoon smoked paprika
- ¾ teaspoon celery salt
- ¾ teaspoon dried mustard
- ½ teaspoon garlic powder
- ½ teaspoon freshly ground black pepper
- ½ teaspoon sea salt
- ½ teaspoon dried thyme
- ¼ teaspoon dried oregano
- 4 large eggs
- Oil spray (hand-pumped)

Directions:

1. Place the chicken and buttermilk in a medium bowl, cover, and refrigerate for at least 1 hour, up to overnight.
2. Preheat the toaster oven to 375°F on AIR FRY for 5 minutes.
3. In a large bowl, stir the flour, paprika, celery salt, mustard, garlic powder, pepper, salt, thyme, and oregano until well mixed.
4. Beat the eggs until frothy in a medium bowl and set them beside the flour.
5. Place the air-fryer basket in the baking tray and generously spray it with the oil.
6. Dredge a chicken drumstick in the flour, then the eggs, and then in the flour again, thickly coating it, and place the drumstick in the basket. Repeat with 5 more drumsticks and spray them all lightly with the oil on all sides.
7. In position 2, air fry for 20 minutes, turning halfway through, until golden brown and crispy with an internal temperature of 165°F.
8. Repeat with the remaining chicken, covering the cooked chicken loosely with foil to keep it warm. Serve.

Jerk Turkey Meatballs

Servings: 7
Cooking Time: 8 Minutes

Ingredients:

- 1 pound lean ground turkey
- ¼ cup chopped onion
- 1 teaspoon minced garlic
- ½ teaspoon dried thyme
- ¼ teaspoon ground cinnamon
- 1 teaspoon cayenne pepper
- ½ teaspoon paprika
- ½ teaspoon salt
- ⅛ teaspoon black pepper
- ¼ teaspoon red pepper flakes
- 2 teaspoons brown sugar
- 1 large egg, whisked
- ⅓ cup panko breadcrumbs
- 2⅓ cups cooked brown Jasmine rice
- 2 green onions, chopped
- ¾ cup sweet onion dressing

Directions:

1. Preheat the toaster oven to 350°F.
2. In a medium bowl, mix the ground turkey with the onion, garlic, thyme, cinnamon, cayenne pepper, paprika, salt, pepper, red pepper flakes, and brown sugar. Add the whisked egg and stir in the breadcrumbs until the turkey starts to hold together.
3. Using a 1-ounce scoop, portion the turkey into meatballs. You should get about 28 meatballs.
4. Spray the air fryer oven with olive oil spray.
5. Place the meatballs into the air fryer oven and air-fry for 5 minutes, rotate the meatball, and cook another 2 to 4 minutes (or until the internal temperature of the meatballs reaches 165°F).
6. Remove the meatballs from the air fryer oven and repeat for the remaining meatballs.
7. Serve warm over a bed of rice with chopped green onions and spicy Caribbean jerk dressing.

Italian Baked Chicken

Servings: 4

Cooking Time: 28 Minutes

Ingredients:

- 1 pound boneless, skinless chicken breasts
- ½ cup dry white wine
- 3 tablespoons olive oil
- 2 tablespoons white wine vinegar
- 2 tablespoons fresh lemon juice
- 2 teaspoons Italian seasoning
- 3 cloves garlic, minced
- ½ teaspoon kosher salt
- ¼ teaspoon freshly ground black pepper
- 4 slices salami, cut in half
- 3 tablespoons shredded Parmesan cheese

Directions:

1. If the chicken breasts are large and thick, slice each breast in half lengthwise. Place the chicken in a shallow baking dish.
2. Combine the white wine, olive oil, vinegar, lemon juice, Italian seasoning, garlic, salt, and pepper in a small bowl. Pour over the chicken breasts. Cover and refrigerate for 2 to 8 hours, turning the chicken occasionally to coat.
3. Preheat the toaster oven to 375 °F.
4. Drain the chicken, discarding the marinade, and place the chicken in an ungreased 12 x 12-inch baking pan. Bake, uncovered, for 20 to 25 minutes or until the chicken is done and a meat thermometer registers 165 °F. Place one slice salami (two pieces) on top of each piece of the chicken. Sprinkle the Parmesan evenly over the chicken breasts and broil for 2 to 3 minutes, or until the cheese is melted and starting to brown.

Crispy "fried" Chicken

Servings: 4
Cooking Time: 14 Minutes

Ingredients:

- ¾ cup all-purpose flour
- ½ teaspoon paprika
- ¼ teaspoon black pepper
- ¼ teaspoon salt
- 2 large eggs
- 1½ cups panko breadcrumbs
- 1 pound boneless, skinless chicken tenders

Directions:

1. Preheat the toaster oven to 400°F.
2. In a shallow bowl, mix the flour with the paprika, pepper, and salt.
3. In a separate bowl, whisk the eggs; set aside.
4. In a third bowl, place the breadcrumbs.
5. Liberally spray the air fryer oven with olive oil spray.
6. Pat the chicken tenders dry with a paper towel. Dredge the tenders one at a time in the flour, then dip them in the egg, and toss them in the breadcrumb coating. Repeat until all tenders are coated.
7. Set each tender in the air fryer oven, leaving room on each side of the tender to allow for flipping.
8. When the air fryer oven is full, cook 4 to 7 minutes, flip, and cook another 4 to 7 minutes.
9. Remove the tenders and let cool 5 minutes before serving. Repeat until all tenders are cooked.

Harissa Lemon Whole Chicken

Servings: 6

Cooking Time: 60 Minutes

Ingredients:
- 2 teaspoons kosher salt
- ½ teaspoon freshly ground black pepper
- ½ teaspoon ground cumin
- 2 garlic cloves
- 6 tablespoons harissa paste
- ½ lemon, juiced
- 1 whole lemon, zested
- 1 (5 pound) whole chicken

Directions:
1. Place salt, pepper, cumin, garlic cloves, harissa paste, lemon juice, and lemon zest in a food processor and pulse until they form a smooth puree.
2. Rub the puree all over the chicken, especially inside the cavity, and cover with plastic wrap.
3. Marinate for 1 hour at room temperature.
4. Preheat the toaster oven to 350°F.
5. Place the marinated chicken on the food tray, then insert the tray at low position in the preheated oven.
6. Select the Roast function, then press Start/Pause.
7. Remove when done, tent chicken with foil, and allow it to rest for 20 minutes before serving.

Chicken Parmesan

Servings: 4
Cooking Time: 11 Minutes

Ingredients:
- 4 chicken tenders
- Italian seasoning
- salt
- ¼ cup cornstarch
- ½ cup Italian salad dressing
- ¼ cup panko breadcrumbs
- ¼ cup grated Parmesan cheese, plus more for serving
- oil for misting or cooking spray
- 8 ounces spaghetti, cooked
- 1 24-ounce jar marinara sauce

Directions:
1. Pound chicken tenders with meat mallet or rolling pin until about ¼-inch thick.
2. Sprinkle both sides with Italian seasoning and salt to taste.
3. Place cornstarch and salad dressing in 2 separate shallow dishes.
4. In a third shallow dish, mix together the panko crumbs and Parmesan cheese.
5. Dip flattened chicken in cornstarch, then salad dressing. Dip in the panko mixture, pressing into the chicken so the coating sticks well.
6. Spray both sides with oil or cooking spray. Place in air fryer oven in single layer.
7. Air-fry at 390°F for 5 minutes. Spray with oil again, turning chicken to coat both sides. See tip about turning.
8. Air-fry for an additional 6 minutes or until chicken juices run clear and outside is browned.
9. While chicken is cooking, heat marinara sauce and stir into cooked spaghetti.
10. To serve, divide spaghetti with sauce among 4 dinner plates, and top each with a fried chicken tender. Pass additional Parmesan at the table for those who want extra cheese.

Jerk Chicken Drumsticks

Servings: 2
Cooking Time: 20 Minutes

Ingredients:

- 1 or 2 cloves garlic
- 1 inch of fresh ginger
- 2 serrano peppers, (with seeds if you like it spicy, seeds removed for less heat)
- 1 teaspoon ground allspice
- 1 teaspoon ground nutmeg
- 1 teaspoon chili powder
- ½ teaspoon dried thyme
- ½ teaspoon ground cinnamon
- ½ teaspoon paprika
- 1 tablespoon brown sugar
- 1 teaspoon soy sauce
- 2 tablespoons vegetable oil
- 6 skinless chicken drumsticks

Directions:

1. Combine all the ingredients except the chicken in a small chopper or blender and blend to a paste. Make slashes into the meat of the chicken drumsticks and rub the spice blend all over the chicken (a pair of plastic gloves makes this really easy). Transfer the rubbed chicken to a non-reactive covered container and let the chicken marinate for at least 30 minutes or overnight in the refrigerator.
2. Preheat the toaster oven to 400°F.
3. Transfer the drumsticks to the air fryer oven. Air-fry for 10 minutes. Turn the drumsticks over and air-fry for another 10 minutes. Serve warm with some rice and vegetables or a green salad.

Rotisserie-style Chicken

Servings: 4
Cooking Time: 75 Minutes

Ingredients:

- 1 (3-pound) whole chicken
- 1 teaspoon sea salt
- 1 teaspoon paprika
- 1 teaspoon dried thyme
- 1 teaspoon dried rosemary
- ¼ teaspoon freshly ground black pepper
- 2 tablespoons olive oil

Directions:

1. Preheat the toaster oven to 375°F on CONVECTION BAKE for 5 minutes.
2. Line the baking tray with foil.
3. Pat the chicken dry with paper towels and season all over with the salt, paprika, thyme, rosemary, and pepper. Place the chicken on the baking tray and drizzle with olive oil.
4. In position 1, bake for 1 hour and 15 minutes, until golden brown and the internal temperature of a thigh reads 165°F.
5. Let the chicken rest for 10 minutes and serve.

Chicken In Mango Sauce

Servings: 2
Cooking Time: 40 Minutes

Ingredients:

- 2 skinless and boneless chicken breast halves
- 1 tablespoon capers
- 1 tablespoon raisins
- Mango mixture:
- 1 cup mango pieces
- 1 teaspoon balsamic vinegar
- ½ teaspoon garlic powder
- 1 teaspoon fresh ginger, peeled and minced
- ½ teaspoon soy sauce
- ½ teaspoon curry powder
- 1 tablespoon pimientos, minced
- Salt and pepper to taste

Directions:

1. Preheat the toaster oven to 375° F.
2. Process the mango mixture ingredients in a food processor or blender until smooth. Transfer to an oiled or nonstick 8½ × 8½ × 2-inch square (cake) pan and add the capers, raisins, and pimientos, stirring well to blend. Add the chicken breasts and spoon the mixture over the breasts to coat well.
3. BAKE for 40 minutes. Serve the breasts with the sauce.

Hot Thighs

Servings: 4

Cooking Time: 40 Minutes

Ingredients:

- 6 skinless, boneless chicken thighs
- ¼ cup fresh lemon juice
- Seasonings:
- 1 teaspoon garlic powder
- ¼ teaspoon cayenne
- ½ teaspoon chili powder
- 1 teaspoon onion powder
- Salt and freshly ground black pepper to taste

Directions:

1. Preheat the toaster oven to 450° F.
2. Brush the chicken thighs liberally with the lemon juice. Set aside.
3. Combine the seasonings in a small bowl and transfer to a paper or plastic bag. Add the thighs and shake well to coat. Remove from the bag and place in an oiled or nonstick 8½ × 8½ × 2-inch square (cake) pan. Cover the pan with aluminum foil.
4. BAKE, covered, for 20 minutes. Turn the pieces with tongs and bake again for another 20 minutes, or until the meat is tender and lightly browned.

Chicken Potpie

Servings: 4
Cooking Time: 48 Minutes

Ingredients:
- Pie filling:
- 1 tablespoon unbleached flour
- ½ cup evaporated skim milk
- 4 skinless, boneless chicken thighs, cut into 1-inch cubes
- 1 cup potatoes, peeled and cut into ½-inch pieces
- ½ cup frozen green peas
- ½ cup thinly sliced carrot
- 2 tablespoons chopped onion
- ½ cup chopped celery
- 1 teaspoon garlic powder
- Salt and freshly ground black pepper to taste
- 8 sheets phyllo pastry, thawed Olive oil

Directions:
1. Preheat the toaster oven to 400° F.
2. Whisk the flour into the milk until smooth in a 1-quart 8½ × 8½ × 4-inch ovenproof baking dish. Add the remaining filling ingredients and mix well. Adjust the seasonings to taste. Cover the dish with aluminum foil.
3. BAKE for 40 minutes, or until the carrot, potatoes, and celery are tender. Remove from the oven and uncover.
4. Place one sheet of phyllo pastry on top of the baked pie-filling mixture, bending the edges to fit the shape of the baking dish. Brush the sheet with olive oil. Add another sheet on top of it and brush with oil. Continue adding the remaining sheets, brushing each one, until the crust is completed. Brush the top with oil.
5. BAKE for 6 minutes, or until the phyllo pastry is browned.

BEEF PORK AND LAMB

Lamb Burger With Feta And Olives

Servings: 3
Cooking Time: 16 Minutes

Ingredients:

- 2 teaspoons olive oil
- ⅓ onion, finely chopped
- 1 clove garlic, minced
- 1 pound ground lamb
- 2 tablespoons fresh parsley, finely chopped
- 1½ teaspoons fresh oregano, finely chopped
- ½ cup black olives, finely chopped
- ⅓ cup crumbled feta cheese
- ½ teaspoon salt
- freshly ground black pepper
- 4 thick pita breads
- toppings and condiments

Directions:

1. Preheat a medium skillet over medium-high heat on the stovetop. Add the olive oil and cook the onion until tender, but not browned – about 4 to 5 minutes. Add the garlic and air-fry for another minute. Transfer the onion and garlic to a mixing bowl and add the ground lamb, parsley, oregano, olives, feta cheese, salt and pepper. Gently mix the ingredients together.

2. Divide the mixture into 3 or 4 equal portions and then form the hamburgers, being careful not to over-handle the meat. One good way to do this is to throw the meat back and forth between your hands like a baseball, packing the meat each time you catch it. Flatten the balls into patties, making an indentation in the center of each patty. Flatten the sides of the patties as well to make it easier to fit them into the air fryer oven.

3. Preheat the toaster oven to 370°F.

4. If you don't have room for all four burgers, air-fry two or three burgers at a time for 8 minutes at 370°F. Flip the burgers over and air-fry for another 8 minutes. If you cooked your burgers in batches, return the first batch of burgers to the air fryer oven for the last two minutes of cooking to re-heat. This should give you a medium-well burger. If you'd prefer a medium-rare burger, shorten the cooking time to about 13 minutes. Remove the burgers to a resting plate and let the burgers rest for a few minutes before dressing and serving.

5. While the burgers are resting, toast the pita breads in the air fryer oven for 2 minutes. Tuck the burgers into the toasted pita breads, or wrap the pitas around the burgers and serve with a tzatziki sauce or some mayonnaise.

Steak With Herbed Butter

Servings: 2

Cooking Time: 16 Minutes

Ingredients:

- 4 tablespoons unsalted butter, softened
- 1 tablespoon minced flat-leaf (Italian) parsley
- 1 tablespoon chopped fresh chives
- 2 cloves garlic, minced
- 1 teaspoon Worcestershire sauce
- 2 beef strip steaks, cut about 1 ½ inches thick
- 1 tablespoon olive oil
- Kosher salt and freshly ground black pepper

Directions:

1. Combine the butter, parsley, chives, garlic, and Worcestershire sauce in a small bowl until well blended; set aside.
2. Preheat the toaster oven to broil.
3. Brush the steaks with olive oil and season with salt and pepper. Place the steak on the broiler rack set over the broiler pan. Place the pan in the toaster oven, positioning the steaks about 3 to 4 inches below the heating element. (Depending on your oven and the thickness of the steak, you may need to set the rack to the middle position.) Broil for 6 minutes, turn the steaks over, and broil for an additional 7 minutes. If necessary to reach the desired doneness, turn the steaks over again and broil for an additional 3 minutes or until you reach your desired doneness.
4. Spread the herb butter generously over the steaks. Allow the steaks to stand for 5 to 10 minutes before slicing and serving.

Meatloaf With Tangy Tomato Glaze

Servings: 6

Cooking Time: 50 Minutes

Ingredients:

- 1 pound ground beef
- ½ pound ground pork
- ½ pound ground veal (or turkey)
- 1 medium onion, diced
- 1 small clove of garlic, minced
- 2 egg yolks, lightly beaten
- ½ cup tomato ketchup
- 1 tablespoon Worcestershire sauce
- ½ cup plain breadcrumbs
- 2 teaspoons salt
- freshly ground black pepper
- ½ cup chopped fresh parsley, plus more for garnish
- 6 tablespoons ketchup
- 1 tablespoon balsamic vinegar
- 2 tablespoons brown sugar

Directions:

1. Combine the meats, onion, garlic, egg yolks, ketchup, Worcestershire sauce, breadcrumbs, salt, pepper and fresh parsley in a large bowl and mix well.
2. Preheat the toaster oven to 350°F and pour a little water into the bottom of the air fryer oven. (This will help prevent the grease that drips into the bottom drawer from burning and smoking.)
3. Transfer the meatloaf mixture to the air fryer oven, packing it down gently. Run a spatula around the meatloaf to create a space about ½-inch wide between the meat and the side of the air fryer oven.
4. Air-fry at 350°F for 20 minutes. Carefully invert the meatloaf onto a plate (remember to remove the pan from the air fryer oven so you don't pour all the grease out) and slide it back into the air fryer oven to turn it over. Re-shape the meatloaf with a spatula if necessary. Air-fry for another 20 minutes at 350°F.
5. Combine the ketchup, balsamic vinegar and brown sugar in a bowl and spread the mixture over the meatloaf. Air-fry for another 10 minutes, until an instant read thermometer inserted into the center of the meatloaf registers 160°F.
6. Allow the meatloaf to rest for a few more minutes and then transfer it to a serving platter using a spatula. Slice the meatloaf, sprinkle a little chopped parsley on top if desired, and serve.

Stuffed Pork Chops

Servings: 4
Cooking Time: 12 Minutes

Ingredients:
- 4 boneless pork chops
- ½ teaspoon salt
- ½ teaspoon black pepper
- ¼ teaspoon paprika
- 1 cup frozen spinach, defrosted and squeezed dry
- 2 cloves garlic, minced
- 2 ounces cream cheese
- ¼ cup grated Parmesan cheese
- 1 tablespoon extra-virgin olive oil

Directions:
1. Pat the pork chops with a paper towel. Make a slit in the side of each pork chop to create a pouch.
2. Season the pork chops with the salt, pepper, and paprika.
3. In a small bowl, mix together the spinach, garlic, cream cheese, and Parmesan cheese.
4. Divide the mixture into fourths and stuff the pork chop pouches. Secure the pouches with toothpicks.
5. Preheat the toaster oven to 400°F.
6. Place the stuffed pork chops in the air fryer oven and spray liberally with cooking spray. Air-fry for 6 minutes, flip and coat with more cooking spray, and cook another 6 minutes. Check to make sure the meat is cooked to an internal temperature of 145°F. Cook the pork chops in batches, as needed.

Italian Meatballs

Servings: 4

Cooking Time: 12 Minutes

Ingredients:

- 12 ounces lean ground beef
- 4 ounces Italian sausage, casing removed
- ½ cup breadcrumbs
- 1 cup grated Parmesan cheese
- 1 egg
- 2 tablespoons milk
- 2 teaspoons Italian seasoning
- ½ teaspoon onion powder
- ½ teaspoon garlic powder
- Pinch of red pepper flakes

Directions:

1. In a large bowl, place all the ingredients and mix well. Roll out 24 meatballs.
2. Preheat the toaster oven to 360°F.
3. Place the meatballs in the air fryer oven and air-fry for 12 minutes, tossing every 4 minutes. Using a food thermometer, check to ensure the internal temperature of the meatballs is 165°F.

Red Curry Flank Steak

Servings: 4
Cooking Time: 18 Minutes

Ingredients:

- 3 tablespoons red curry paste
- ¼ cup olive oil
- 2 teaspoons grated fresh ginger
- 2 tablespoons soy sauce
- 2 tablespoons rice wine vinegar
- 3 scallions, minced
- 1½ pounds flank steak
- fresh cilantro (or parsley) leaves

Directions:

1. Mix the red curry paste, olive oil, ginger, soy sauce, rice vinegar and scallions together in a bowl. Place the flank steak in a shallow glass dish and pour half the marinade over the steak. Pierce the steak several times with a fork or meat tenderizer to let the marinade penetrate the meat. Turn the steak over, pour the remaining marinade over the top and pierce the steak several times again. Cover and marinate the steak in the refrigerator for 6 to 8 hours.

2. When you are ready to cook, remove the steak from the refrigerator and let it sit at room temperature for 30 minutes.

3. Preheat the toaster oven to 400°F.

4. Cut the flank steak in half so that it fits more easily into the air fryer oven and transfer both pieces to the air fryer oven. Pour the marinade over the steak. Air-fry for 18 minutes, depending on your preferred degree of doneness of the steak (12 minutes = medium rare). Flip the steak over halfway through the cooking time.

5. When your desired degree of doneness has been reached, remove the steak to a cutting board and let it rest for 5 minutes before slicing. Thinly slice the flank steak against the grain of the meat. Transfer the slices to a serving platter, pour any juice from the bottom of the air fryer oven over the sliced flank steak and sprinkle the fresh cilantro on top.

Beef-stuffed Bell Peppers

Servings: 4

Cooking Time: 30 Minutes

Ingredients:

- 4 medium red or yellow bell peppers
- 1 pound extra-lean ground beef
- ½ sweet onion, finely chopped
- 2 teaspoons minced garlic
- 1 cup marinara sauce
- 1 cup ready-made brown or wild rice
- 1 cup fresh kale, chopped
- 1 teaspoon dried basil
- Sea salt, for seasoning
- Freshly ground black pepper, for seasoning
- 1 cup Swiss cheese, shredded

Directions:

1. Preheat the toaster oven to 350°F on AIR FRY for 5 minutes.
2. Cut the top off the peppers and scoop the seeds and membranes out. Set the pepper tops aside.
3. Place a large skillet over medium-high heat and brown the beef, about 10 minutes.
4. Add the onion and garlic and sauté until softened, about 4 minutes.
5. Add the marinara sauce, rice, kale, and basil, stirring to combine. Remove from the heat and season with salt and pepper.
6. Place the air-fryer basket in the baking tray and place the peppers in the basket, hollow-side up.
7. Evenly divide the filling among the peppers. You can place the pepper tops cut-side up and place the pepper bottoms in the tops to balance them, so that they do not tip over.
8. In position 1, air fry for 15 minutes until the peppers are tender. Top with the cheese and air fry for 2 more minutes more to melt the cheese. Serve.

Ribeye Steak With Blue Cheese Compound Butter

Servings: 2

Cooking Time: 12 Minutes

Ingredients:

- 5 tablespoons unsalted butter, softened
- ¼ cup crumbled blue cheese 2 teaspoons lemon juice
- 1 tablespoon freshly chopped chives
- Salt & freshly ground black pepper, to taste
- 2 (12 ounce) boneless ribeye steaks

Directions:

1. Mix together butter, blue cheese, lemon juice, and chives until smooth.
2. Season the butter to taste with salt and pepper.
3. Place the butter on plastic wrap and form into a 3-inch log, tying the ends of the plastic wrap together.
4. Place the butter in the fridge for 4 hours to harden.
5. Allow the steaks to sit at room temperature for 1 hour.
6. Pat the steaks dry with paper towels and season to taste with salt and pepper.
7. Insert the fry basket at top position in the Cosori Smart Air Fryer Toaster Oven.
8. Preheat the toaster Oven to 450°F.
9. Place the steaks in the fry basket in the preheated oven.
10. Select the Broil function, adjust time to 12 minutes, and press Start/Pause.
11. Remove when done and allow to rest for 5 minutes.
12. Remove the butter from the fridge, unwrap, and slice into ¾-inch pieces.
13. Serve the steak with one or two pieces of sliced compound butter.

Skirt Steak Fajitas

Servings: 4
Cooking Time: 30 Minutes

Ingredients:

- 2 tablespoons olive oil
- ¼ cup lime juice
- 1 clove garlic, minced
- ½ teaspoon ground cumin
- ½ teaspoon hot sauce
- ½ teaspoon salt
- 2 tablespoons chopped fresh cilantro
- 1 pound skirt steak
- 1 onion, sliced
- 1 teaspoon chili powder
- 1 red pepper, sliced
- 1 green pepper, sliced
- salt and freshly ground black pepper
- 8 flour tortillas
- shredded lettuce, crumbled Queso Fresco (or grated Cheddar cheese), sliced black olives, diced tomatoes, sour cream and guacamole for serving

Directions:

1. Combine the olive oil, lime juice, garlic, cumin, hot sauce, salt and cilantro in a shallow dish. Add the skirt steak and turn it over several times to coat all sides. Pierce the steak with a needle-style meat tenderizer or paring knife. Marinate the steak in the refrigerator for at least 3 hours, or overnight. When you are ready to cook, remove the steak from the refrigerator and let it sit at room temperature for 30 minutes.

2. Preheat the toaster oven to 400°F.

3. Toss the onion slices with the chili powder and a little olive oil and transfer them to the air fryer oven. Air-fry at 400°F for 5 minutes. Add the red and green peppers to the air fryer oven with the onions, season with salt and pepper and air-fry for 8 more minutes, until the onions and peppers are soft. Transfer the vegetables to a dish and cover with aluminum foil to keep warm.

4. Place the skirt steak in the air fryer oven and pour the marinade over the top. Air-fry at 400°F for 12 minutes. Flip the steak over and air-fry at 400°F for an additional 5 minutes. (The time needed for your steak will depend on the thickness of the skirt steak. 17 minutes should bring your steak to roughly medium.) Transfer the cooked steak to a cutting board and let the steak rest for a few minutes. If the peppers and onions need to be heated, return them to the air fryer oven for just 1 to 2 minutes.

5. Thinly slice the steak at an angle, cutting against the grain of the steak. Serve the steak with the onions and peppers, the warm tortillas and the fajita toppings on the side so that everyone can make their own fajita.

Cilantro-crusted Flank Steak

Servings: 2
Cooking Time: 16 Minutes

Ingredients:
- Coating:
- 2 tablespoons chopped onion
- 1 tablespoon olive oil
- 2 tablespoons plain nonfat yogurt
- 1 plum tomato
- ½ cup fresh cilantro leaves
- 2 tablespoons cooking sherry
- ¼ teaspoon hot sauce
- 1 teaspoon garlic powder
- ½ teaspoon chili powder
- Salt and freshly ground black pepper
- 2 8-ounce flank steaks

Directions:
1. Process the coating ingredients in a blender or food processor until smooth. Spread half of the coating mixture on top of the flank steaks. Place the steaks on a broiling rack with a pan underneath.
2. BROIL for 8 minutes. Turn with tongs, spread the remaining mixture on the steaks, and broil again for 8 minutes, or until done to your preference.

Easy Tex-mex Chimichangas

Servings: 2
Cooking Time: 8 Minutes

Ingredients:

- ¼ pound Thinly sliced deli roast beef, chopped
- ½ cup (about 2 ounces) Shredded Cheddar cheese or shredded Tex-Mex cheese blend
- ¼ cup Jarred salsa verde or salsa rojo
- ½ teaspoon Ground cumin
- ½ teaspoon Dried oregano
- 2 Burrito-size (12-inch) flour tortilla(s), not corn tortillas (gluten-free, if a concern)
- ⅔ cup Canned refried beans
- Vegetable oil spray

Directions:

1. Preheat the toaster oven to 375°F .
2. Stir the roast beef, cheese, salsa, cumin, and oregano in a bowl until well mixed.
3. Lay a tortilla on a clean, dry work surface. Spread ⅓ cup of the refried beans in the center lower third of the tortilla(s), leaving an inch on either side of the spread beans.
4. For one chimichanga, spread all of the roast beef mixture on top of the beans. For two, spread half of the roast beef mixture on each tortilla.
5. At either "end" of the filling mixture, fold the sides of the tortilla up and over the filling, partially covering it. Starting with the unfolded side of the tortilla just below the filling, roll the tortilla closed. Fold and roll the second filled tortilla, as necessary.
6. Coat the exterior of the tortilla(s) with vegetable oil spray. Set the chimichanga(s) seam side down in the air fryer oven, with at least ½ inch air space between them if you're working with two. Air-fry undisturbed for 8 minutes, or until the tortilla is lightly browned and crisp.
7. Use kitchen tongs to gently transfer the chimichanga(s) to a wire rack. Cool for at last 5 minutes or up to 20 minutes before serving.

DESSERTS

Warm Chocolate Fudge Cakes

Servings: 2
Cooking Time: 35 Minutes

Ingredients:

- 6 tablespoons (1¾ ounces) all-purpose flour
- ¼ teaspoon baking powder
- ⅛ teaspoon baking soda
- ⅛ teaspoon table salt
- 2½ ounces bittersweet chocolate (2 ounces chopped, ½ ounce cut into ½-inch pieces)
- ¼ cup whole milk, room temperature
- 3 tablespoons packed light brown sugar
- 2 tablespoons vegetable oil
- 1 large egg, lightly beaten
- ¼ teaspoon vanilla extract

Directions:

1. Adjust toaster oven rack to middle position and preheat the toaster oven to 350 degrees. Grease and flour two 6-ounce ramekins. Whisk flour, baking powder, baking soda, and salt together in bowl.

2. Microwave chopped chocolate and milk in medium bowl at 50 percent power, stirring occasionally, until chocolate is melted and mixture is smooth, 1 to 3 minutes. Stir in sugar until dissolved; let cool slightly. Whisk in oil, egg, and vanilla until combined. Gently whisk in flour mixture until just combined.

3. Divide batter evenly between prepared ramekins and gently tap each ramekin on counter to release air bubbles. Wipe any drops of batter off sides of ramekins. Gently press chocolate pieces evenly into center of each ramekin to submerge in batter. Place ramekins on small rimmed baking sheet and bake cakes until tops are just firm to touch and center is gooey when pierced with toothpick, 10 to 15 minutes. Let cool for 2 to 3 minutes before serving.

Coconut Rice Pudding

Servings: 6
Cooking Time: 55 Minutes

Ingredients:

- ½ cup short-grain brown rice
- Pudding mixture:
- 1 egg, beaten
- 1 tablespoon cornstarch
- ½ cup fat-free half-and-half
- ½ cup chopped raisins
- 1 teaspoon vanilla extract
- ½ teaspoon ground cinnamon
- ½ teaspoon grated nutmeg
- Salt to taste
- ¼ cup shredded sweetened coconut
- Fat-free whipped topping

Directions:

1. Preheat the toaster oven to 400° F.
2. Combine the rice and 1½ cups water in a 1-quart 8½ × 8½ × 4-inch ovenproof baking dish. Cover with aluminum foil.
3. BAKE, covered, for 45 minutes, or until the rice is tender. Remove from the oven and add the pudding mixture ingredients, mixing well.
4. BAKE, uncovered, for 10 minutes, or until the top is lightly browned. Sprinkle the top with coconut and chill before serving. Top with fat-free whipped topping.

Bourbon Bread Pudding

Servings: 2
Cooking Time: 120 Minutes

Ingredients:

- 6 ounces baguette, torn into 1-inch pieces (4 cups)
- ¼ cup raisins
- 2 tablespoons bourbon
- ¾ cup heavy cream
- ⅓ cup packed (2⅓ ounces) light brown sugar
- ¼ cup whole milk
- 2 large egg yolks
- 1 teaspoon vanilla extract
- ½ teaspoon ground cinnamon, divided
- ⅛ teaspoon table salt
- Pinch ground nutmeg
- 2 tablespoons unsalted butter, cut into ¼-inch pieces
- 1 tablespoon granulated sugar

Directions:

1. Adjust toaster oven rack to middle position and preheat the toaster oven to 375 degrees. Spread bread in single layer on small rimmed baking sheet and bake until golden brown and crisp, 10 to 20 minutes, tossing halfway through baking. Let bread cool completely.

2. Meanwhile, microwave raisins and bourbon in covered bowl until bubbling, 30 to 60 seconds. Let sit until softened, about 15 minutes.

3. Whisk cream, brown sugar, milk, egg yolks, vanilla, ¼ teaspoon cinnamon, salt, and nutmeg together in large bowl. Add bread and raisin mixture and toss until evenly coated. Let mixture sit, tossing occasionally, until bread begins to absorb custard and is softened, about 20 minutes.

4. Grease two 12-ounce ramekins. Divide bread mixture evenly between prepared ramekins and sprinkle with butter, granulated sugar, and remaining ¼ teaspoon cinnamon. Cover each ramekin with aluminum foil, place on small rimmed baking sheet, and bake for 30 minutes.

5. Remove foil from bread puddings and continue to bake until tops are crisp and golden brown, 10 to 15 minutes. Let bread puddings cool for 15 minutes before serving.

Cowboy Cookies

Servings: 3

Cooking Time: 14 Minutes

Ingredients:

- Recommended Hamilton Beach® Product: Stand Mixers
- 1 cup butter
- 1 cup sugar
- 1 cup light brown sugar
- 2 eggs
- 2 cups flour
- 1 teaspoon baking soda
- ½ teaspoon baking powder
- ½ teaspoon salt
- 2 cups oatmeal
- 1 tablespoon vanilla
- 12 ounces chocolate chips
- 1 ½ cups coconut

Directions:

1. Preheat the toaster oven to 350°F.
2. With flat beater attachment, cream together butter, sugar, and brown sugar at a medium setting until well blended. Mix in vanilla and eggs. Reduce speed and gradually add flour, baking soda, baking powder, and salt mix until smooth.
3. On a low setting, mix in oatmeal, chocolate chips, and coconut until well mixed. Drop rounded spoon full onto ungreased cookie sheet.
4. Bake on middle rack of oven for 12 to 14 minutes.

Buttermilk Confetti Cake

Servings: 10-12
Cooking Time: 25 Minutes

Ingredients:
- 1 1/2 cups all purpose flour
- 1/2 teaspoon baking soda
- 1/4 teaspoon salt
- 1/2 cup butter, softened
- 1 cup sugar
- 1 teaspoon vanilla extract
- 2 large eggs
- 3/4 cup buttermilk
- 1/4 cup multi-colored sprinkle
- Cream Cheese Frosting
- Multi-colored sprinkles

Directions:
1. Preheat the toaster oven to 350°F. Grease two 8-inch cake pans and line with parchment paper.
2. Stir flour, baking soda and salt in small bowl. Set mixture aside.
3. Beat butter, sugar and vanilla extract on HIGH in large bowl until blended. Add eggs, one at a time, until well blended.
4. Alternately add flour mixture and buttermilk until combined. Stir in 1/4 cup sprinkles.
5. Divide batter evenly between prepared pans. Place one pan on bottom rack and one pan on top rack, rotate halfway through baking.
6. Bake 20 to 25 minutes or until a toothpick inserted in center of cakes comes out clean. Cool 10 minutes on wire rack.
7. Remove cakes from pans and cool completely on wire racks. Frost with Cream Cheese Frosting and top with sprinkles.

Blackberry Pie

Servings: 6
Cooking Time: 30 Minutes

Ingredients:

- Filling:
- 2 16-ounce bags frozen blackberries, thawed, or 2 cups fresh blackberries, washed and well drained
- 1 4-ounce jar baby food prunes
- 2 tablespoons cornstarch
- 3 ¼ cup brown sugar
- 1 tablespoon lemon juice
- Salt to taste
- 1 Graham Cracker Crust, baked (recipe follows)
- Meringue Topping (recipe follows)

Directions:

1. Preheat the toaster oven to 350° F.
2. Combine the filling ingredients in a large bowl, mixing well. Spoon the filling into the baked Graham Cracker Crust and spread evenly.
3. BAKE for 30 minutes. When cool, top with the Meringue Topping.

Graham Cracker Crust

Servings: 4
Cooking Time: 14 Minutes

Ingredients:
- 1⅓ cups reduced-fat graham cracker crumbs
- 2 tablespoons brown sugar
- 1 teaspoon ground cinnamon
- Salt to taste
- 1 tablespoon margarine
- 2 tablespoons vegetable oil

Directions:
1. Process the graham crackers in a food processor or blender to produce finely ground crumbs. Add the sugar, cinnamon, and salt and blend by stirring. Set aside.
2. Heat the margarine and oil under a broiler for 4 minutes, or until the margarine is almost melted. Remove from the oven and stir until the margarine is completely melted. Add the graham cracker crumbs and mix thoroughly.
3. Press the mixture into a 9¾-inch pie pan, spreading it out evenly from the middle and up the sides of the pan.
4. BAKE at 350° F. for 10 minutes, or until lightly browned. Cool before filling.

Midnight Nutella® Banana Sandwich

Servings: 2
Cooking Time: 8 Minutes

Ingredients:

- butter, softened
- 4 slices white bread
- ¼ cup chocolate hazelnut spread (Nutella®)
- 1 banana

Directions:

1. Preheat the toaster oven to 370°F.

2. Spread the softened butter on one side of all the slices of bread and place the slices buttered side down on the counter. Spread the chocolate hazelnut spread on the other side of the bread slices. Cut the banana in half and then slice each half into three slices lengthwise. Place the banana slices on two slices of bread and top with the remaining slices of bread (buttered side up) to make two sandwiches. Cut the sandwiches in half (triangles or rectangles) – this will help them all fit in the air fryer oven at once. Transfer the sandwiches to the air fryer oven.

3. Air-fry at 370°F for 5 minutes. Flip the sandwiches over and air-fry for another 2 to 3 minutes, or until the top bread slices are nicely browned. Pour yourself a glass of milk or a midnight nightcap while the sandwiches cool slightly and enjoy!

Blueberry Crisp

Servings: 6

Cooking Time: 13 Minutes

Ingredients:

- 3 cups Fresh or thawed frozen blueberries
- ⅓ cup Granulated white sugar
- 1 tablespoon Instant tapioca
- ⅓ cup All-purpose flour
- ⅓ cup Rolled oats (not quick-cooking or steel-cut)
- ⅓ cup Chopped walnuts or pecans
- ⅓ cup Packed light brown sugar
- 5 tablespoons plus 1 teaspoon (⅔ stick) Butter, melted and cooled
- ¾ teaspoon Ground cinnamon
- ¼ teaspoon Table salt

Directions:

1. Preheat the toaster oven to 400°F.
2. Mix the blueberries, granulated white sugar, and instant tapioca in a 6-inch round cake pan for a small batch, a 7-inch round cake pan for a medium batch, or an 8-inch round cake pan for a large batch.
3. When the machine is at temperature, set the cake pan in the air fryer oven and air-fry undisturbed for 5 minutes, or just until the blueberries begin to bubble.
4. Meanwhile, mix the flour, oats, nuts, brown sugar, butter, cinnamon, and salt in a medium bowl until well combined.
5. When the blueberries have begun to bubble, crumble this flour mixture evenly on top. Continue air-frying undisturbed for 8 minutes, or until the topping has browned a bit and the filling is bubbling.
6. Use two hot pads or silicone baking mitts to transfer the cake pan to a wire rack. Cool for at least 10 minutes or to room temperature before serving.

Almond Amaretto Bundt Cake

Servings: 8
Cooking Time: 37 Minutes

Ingredients:

- Nonstick baking spray with flour
- 1 (15.25- to 18-ounce) box yellow cake mix
- 1 (3.9-ounce) box vanilla instant pudding
- 1 cup sour cream
- ½ cup canola or vegetable oil
- ¼ cup amaretto or almond liqueur
- 4 large eggs
- ¼ teaspoon pure almond extract
- GLAZE
- 2 ½ cups confectioners' sugar
- 2 tablespoons amaretto
- 1 teaspoon pure vanilla extract
- 1 to 2 tablespoons milk
- Sliced almonds, toasted

Directions:

1. Preheat the toaster oven to 350°F. Spray a 12-cup Bundt pan with nonstick baking spray with flour.
2. Beat the cake mix, instant pudding, sour cream, oil, ¼ cup water, the amaretto, eggs, and almond extract in a large bowl with a handheld mixer at low speed for 30 seconds to combine the ingredients. Scrape the sides of the bowl with a rubber scraper. Beat on medium-high speed for 2 minutes.
3. Pour the batter into the prepared pan. Bake for 30 to 35 minutes, or until a wooden pick inserted into the center comes out clean.
4. Place the pan on a wire rack to cool for 10 minutes. Invert the cake onto the rack and let cool completely.
5. Meanwhile, make the glaze: Whisk the sugar, amaretto, vanilla, and 1 tablespoon milk in a small bowl. If needed, stir in the additional milk to make the desired consistency. Pour over the cake. Garnish with the sliced almonds.

Coconut Cake

Servings: 6
Cooking Time: 25 Minutes

Ingredients:

- 2 cups unbleached flour
- 2 teaspoons baking powder
- 1 cup skim or low-fat soy milk
- 2 tablespoons vegetable oil
- 3 1 teaspoon vanilla extract
- 1 egg, beaten
- ¾ cup sugar
- Salt to taste
- Creamy Frosting (recipe follows)

Directions:

1. Preheat the toaster oven to 350° F.
2. Combine all the ingredients in a large bowl, mixing well.
3. Pour the cake batter into an oiled or nonstick 8½ × 8½ × 2-inch square baking (cake) pan.
4. BAKE for 25 minutes, or until a toothpick inserted in the center comes out clean. Ice with Creamy Frosting and sprinkle with coconut.

SNACKS APPETIZERS AND SIDES

Korean "fried" Chicken Wings

Servings: 4
Cooking Time: 25 Minutes

Ingredients:

- Wings Ingredients
- 2 pounds chicken wings
- 1 teaspoon kosher salt
- ½ teaspoon black pepper
- 1½ teaspoons onion powder
- 1½ teaspoons garlic powder
- ¾ teaspoons ground mustard
- 1 teaspoon gochugaru
- 2 tablespoons cornstarch
- 1 tablespoon water
- Cooking spray
- Toasted sesame seeds, for sprinkling
- Sauce Ingredients
- 3 tablespoons Korean gojuchang red pepper paste
- 2 tablespoon white distilled vinegar
- 1 tablespoon hot water
- 2 tablespoons honey
- 1 tablespoon soy sauce

Directions:

1. Combine all the ingredients for the wings except the cooking spray and sesame seeds in a large bowl. Mix well.
2. Preheat the toaster oven to 400°F.
3. Spray both sides of the wings with cooking spray.
4. Place the wings into the fry basket, then insert the basket at mid position in the preheated oven.
5. Select the Air Fry function, adjust time to 25 minutes, then press Start/Pause.
6. Mix together sauce ingredients until well combined, then microwave on high for 30 seconds. Set aside.
7. Remove wings when done, then place the wings and sauce in a large bowl and toss together until the wings are well coated.
8. Sprinkle the wings with toasted sesame seeds and serve.

Middle Eastern Phyllo Rolls

Servings: 6

Cooking Time: 5 Minutes

Ingredients:

- 6 ounces Lean ground beef or ground lamb
- 3 tablespoons Sliced almonds
- 1 tablespoon Chutney (any variety), finely chopped
- ¼ teaspoon Ground cinnamon
- ¼ teaspoon Ground coriander
- ¼ teaspoon Ground cumin
- ¼ teaspoon Ground dried turmeric
- ¼ teaspoon Table salt
- ¼ teaspoon Ground black pepper
- 6 18 × 14-inch phyllo sheets (thawed, if necessary)
- Olive oil spray

Directions:

1. Set a medium skillet over medium heat for a minute or two, then crumble in the ground meat. Air-fry for 3 minutes, stirring often, or until well browned. Stir in the almonds, chutney, cinnamon, coriander, cumin, turmeric, salt, and pepper until well combined. Remove from the heat, scrape the cooked ground meat mixture into a bowl, and cool for 15 minutes.
2. Preheat the toaster oven to 400°F.
3. Place one sheet of phyllo dough on a clean, dry work surface. (Keep the others covered.) Lightly coat it with olive oil spray, then fold it in half by bringing the short ends together. Place about 3 tablespoons of the ground meat mixture along one of the longer edges, then fold both of the shorter sides of the dough up and over the meat to partially enclose it (and become a border along the sheet of dough). Roll the dough closed, coat it with olive oil spray on all sides, and set it aside seam side down. Repeat this filling and spraying process with the remaining phyllo sheets.
4. Set the rolls seam side down in the air fryer oven in one layer with some air space between them. Air-fry undisturbed for 5 minutes, or until very crisp and golden brown.
5. Use kitchen tongs to transfer the rolls to a wire rack. Cool for only 2 or 3 minutes before serving hot.

Baked Asparagus Fries

Servings: 2-3
Cooking Time: 14 Minutes

Ingredients:
- 1 1/2 cups mayonnaise
- 3/4 cup grated Parmesan cheese
- 2 cloves garlic, minced
- 1 tablespoon dried parsley
- 1 tablespoon Italian seasoning
- 1 teaspoon salt
- 1/2 teaspoon coarse black pepper
- 1/2 pound thick asparagus, trimmed
- 1 cup panko crumbs

Directions:
1. Heat the oven to 425°F.
2. In a small bowl, combine mayonnaise, Parmesan cheese, garlic, parsley, Italian seasoning, salt and black pepper.
3. Brush asparagus with 3 tablespoons mayonnaise mixture and roll in crumbs. Place asparagus on the baking pan.
4. Bake 12 to 14 minutes or until lightly browned and asparagus are cooked.
5. Serve asparagus with the remaining mayonnaise mixture.

Loaded Potato Skins

Servings: 8
Cooking Time: 8 Minutes

Ingredients:

- 12 round baby potatoes
- 3 ounces cream cheese
- 4 slices cooked bacon, crumbled or chopped
- 2 green onions, finely chopped
- ½ cup grated cheddar cheese, divided
- ¼ cup sour cream
- 1 tablespoon milk
- 2 teaspoons hot sauce

Directions:

1. Preheat the toaster oven to 320°F.
2. Poke holes into the baby potatoes with a fork. Place the potatoes onto a microwave-safe plate and microwave on high for 4 to 5 minutes, or until soft to squeeze. Let the potatoes cool until they're safe to handle, about 5 minutes.
3. Meanwhile, in a medium bowl, mix together the cream cheese, bacon, green onions, and ¼ cup of the cheddar cheese; set aside.
4. Slice the baby potatoes in half. Using a spoon, scoop out the pulp, leaving enough pulp on the inside to retain the shape of the potato half. Place the potato pulp into the cream cheese mixture and mash together with a fork. Using a spoon, refill the potato halves with filling.
5. Place the potato halves into the air fryer oven and top with the remaining ¼ cup of cheddar cheese.
6. Cook the loaded baked potato bites in batches for 8 minutes.
7. Meanwhile, make the sour cream sauce. In a small bowl, whisk together the sour cream, milk, and hot sauce. Add more hot sauce if desired.
8. When the potatoes have all finished cooking, place them onto a serving platter and serve with sour cream sauce drizzled over the top or as a dip.

Beef Empanadas

Servings: 8

Cooking Time: 75 Minutes

Ingredients:

- 8 ounces 93 percent lean ground beef
- 3 garlic cloves, minced
- 2 teaspoons chili powder
- 1 teaspoon ground cumin
- 1 teaspoon minced fresh oregano or ¼ teaspoon dried
- 4 ounces Monterey Jack cheese, shredded (1 cup)
- 1 cup mild tomato salsa, drained
- 2 tablespoons chopped fresh cilantro
- 1 package store-bought pie dough
- 1 large egg, lightly beaten

Directions:

1. Microwave beef, garlic, chili powder, cumin, and oregano in bowl, stirring occasionally and breaking up meat with wooden spoon, until beef is no longer pink, about 3 minutes. Transfer beef mixture to fine-mesh strainer set over large bowl and let drain for 10 minutes; discard juices. Return drained beef mixture to now-empty bowl and stir in Monterey Jack, salsa, and cilantro.

2. Adjust toaster oven rack to middle position, select air-fry or convection setting, and preheat the toaster oven to 350 degrees. Line large and small rimmed baking sheets with parchment paper. Roll 1 dough round into 12-inch circle on lightly floured counter. Using 5-inch round biscuit cutter, stamp out 4 rounds; discard dough scraps. Repeat with remaining dough round. Mound beef mixture evenly in center of each stamped round. Fold dough over filling and crimp edges together with fork to seal.

3. Space desired number of empanadas at least 1 inch apart on prepared small sheet; space remaining empanadas evenly on prepared large sheet. Brush all empanadas with egg.

4. Cook small sheet of empanadas until golden brown and crisp, 15 to 25 minutes. Transfer empanadas to wire rack and let cool for 15 minutes before serving.

5. Freeze remaining large sheet of empanadas until firm, about 1 hour. Transfer empanadas to 1-gallon zipper-lock bag and freeze for up to 1 month. Cook frozen empanadas as directed; do not thaw.

Polenta Fries With Chili-lime Mayo

Servings: 4

Cooking Time: 28 Minutes

Ingredients:

- 2 teaspoons vegetable or olive oil
- ¼ teaspoon paprika
- 1 pound prepared polenta, cut into 3-inch x ½-inch sticks
- salt and freshly ground black pepper
- Chili-Lime Mayo
- ½ cup mayonnaise
- 1 teaspoon chili powder
- ¼ teaspoon ground cumin
- juice of half a lime
- 1 teaspoon chopped fresh cilantro
- salt and freshly ground black pepper

Directions:

1. Preheat the toaster oven to 400°F.
2. Combine the oil and paprika and then carefully toss the polenta sticks in the mixture.
3. Air-fry the polenta fries at 400°F for 15 minutes. Rotate the fries and continue to air-fry for another 13 minutes or until the fries have browned nicely. Season to taste with salt and freshly ground black pepper.
4. To make the chili-lime mayo, combine all the ingredients in a small bowl and stir well.
5. Serve the polenta fries warm with chili-lime mayo on the side for dipping.

Baked Coconut Shrimp With Curried Chutney

Servings: 8-10

Cooking Time: 11 Minutes

Ingredients:
- 1 cup chutney
- 2 Tablespoons sliced green onion
- 1/2 teaspoon ground curry
- 1/2 teaspoon crushed red pepper
- 2 Tablespoons all-purpose flour
- 1 teaspoon salt
- 1 cup panko breadcrumbs
- 3/4 cup sweetened shredded coconut
- 1 egg white
- 1 pound (16 to 20 count) extra jumbo shrimp
- Cilantro

Directions:
1. In a small bowl, stir chutney, green onion, curry and crushed red pepper until blended. Set aside.
2. Preheat the toaster oven to 450°F. Spray a baking pan with nonstick cooking spray. Set aside.
3. In a large resealable plastic bag, combine flour and salt.
4. Add panko breadcrumbs and coconut to bag. Seal and shake to combine.
5. In a medium bowl, whisk egg white until foamy.
6. Dip one shrimp at a time into egg white.
7. Place shrimp in crumb mixture and press mixture onto shrimp until well coated. Arrange in single layer in prepared baking pan.
8. Bake for 9 to 11 minutes or until crumbs are golden brown. Serve with chutney mixture. Garnish with cilantro.

Corn Dog Muffins

Servings: 8
Cooking Time: 10 Minutes

Ingredients:

- 1¼ cups sliced kosher hotdogs (3 or 4, depending on size)
- ½ cup flour
- ½ cup yellow cornmeal
- 2 teaspoons baking powder
- ½ cup skim milk
- 1 egg
- 2 tablespoons canola oil
- 8 foil muffin cups, paper liners removed
- cooking spray
- mustard or your favorite dipping sauce

Directions:

1. Slice each hot dog in half lengthwise, then cut in ¼-inch half-moon slices. Set aside.
2. Preheat the toaster oven to 390°F.
3. In a large bowl, stir together flour, cornmeal, and baking powder.
4. In a small bowl, beat together the milk, egg, and oil until just blended.
5. Pour egg mixture into dry ingredients and stir with a spoon to mix well.
6. Stir in sliced hot dogs.
7. Spray the foil cups lightly with cooking spray.
8. Divide mixture evenly into muffin cups.
9. Place 4 muffin cups in the air fryer oven and air-fry for 5 minutes.
10. Reduce temperature to 360°F and cook 5 minutes or until toothpick inserted in center of muffin comes out clean.
11. Repeat steps 9 and 10 to bake remaining corn dog muffins.
12. Serve with mustard or other sauces for dipping.

Cheesy Zucchini Squash Casserole

Servings: 12-14

Cooking Time: 30 Minutes

Ingredients:

- 1 Tablespoon olive oil
- 1 medium sweet onion, halved and thinly sliced
- 1 garlic clove, minced
- 1 pound zucchini, thinly sliced
- 1 pound yellow squash, thinly sliced
- 1 large egg
- 1/2 cup sour cream
- 1 cup shredded Cheddar cheese
- 1 cup shredded Swiss cheese
- 1 teaspoon thyme
- 1 teaspoon salt
- 1/2 teaspoon black pepper
- 3/4 cup seasoned panko crumbs
- 1 Tablespoon butter, melted

Directions:

1. Preheat the toaster oven to 350°F.
2. Heat olive oil in large skillet over medium-high heat. Add onion and garlic; cook 2 minutes. Stir in zucchini and yellow squash, cooking an additional 4 minutes or until squash is tender.
3. Beat egg and sour cream in large bowl until well blended. Stir in squash mixture, cheeses, thyme, salt and pepper. Pour into 8x8-inch baking dish.
4. Stir crumbs and butter in small bowl. Sprinkle over squash mixture.
5. Bake 25 to 30 minutes or until crumbs are golden brown and mixture is heated through.

Sweet Or Savory Baked Sweet Potatoes

Servings: 6
Cooking Time: 60 Minutes

Ingredients:

- 6 medium sweet potatoes, scrubbed
- Cinnamon Butter
- Salted Garlic Herb Butter

Directions:

1. Preheat the toaster oven to 450ºF. Line a 15x10-inch baking pan with foil.

2. Prick each sweet potato several times with a fork and place on baking pan.

3. Bake 45 to 1 hour or until fork tender. Serve with Cinnamon Butter or Salted Garlic Herb Butter.

Buffalo Bites

Servings: 16
Cooking Time: 12 Minutes

Ingredients:
- 1 pound ground chicken
- 8 tablespoons buffalo wing sauce
- 2 ounces Gruyère cheese, cut into 16 cubes
- 1 tablespoon maple syrup

Directions:
1. Mix 4 tablespoons buffalo wing sauce into all the ground chicken.
2. Shape chicken into a log and divide into 16 equal portions.
3. With slightly damp hands, mold each chicken portion around a cube of cheese and shape into a firm ball. When you have shaped 8 meatballs, place them in air fryer oven.
4. Air-fry at 390°F for approximately 5 minutes. Reduce temperature to 360°F, and air-fry for 5 minutes longer.
5. While the first batch is cooking, shape remaining chicken and cheese into 8 more meatballs.
6. Repeat step 4 to cook second batch of meatballs.
7. In a medium bowl, mix the remaining 4 tablespoons of buffalo wing sauce with the maple syrup. Add all the cooked meatballs and toss to coat.
8. Place meatballs back into air fryer oven and air-fry at 390°F for 2 minutes to set the glaze. Skewer each with a toothpick and serve.

VEGETABLES AND VEGETARIAN

Eggplant And Tomato Slices

Servings: 4
Cooking Time: 36 Minutes

Ingredients:
- 2 tablespoons olive oil
- ¼ teaspoon garlic powder
- 4 ½-inch-thick slices eggplant
- 4 ¼-inch-thick slices fresh tomato
- 2 tablespoons tomato sauce or salsa
- ½ cup shredded Parmesan cheese
- Salt and freshly ground black pepper to taste
- 2 tablespoons chopped fresh basil, cilantro, parsley, or oregano

Directions:
1. Whisk together the oil and garlic powder in a small bowl. Brush each eggplant slice with the mixture and place in an oiled or nonstick 8½ × 8½ × 2-inch square baking (cake) pan.
2. BROIL for 20 minutes. Remove the pan from the oven and turn the pieces with tongs. Top each with a slice of tomato and broil another 10 minutes, or until tender. Remove the pan from the oven, brush each slice with tomato sauce or salsa, and sprinkle generously with Parmesan cheese. Season to taste with salt and pepper. Broil again for 6 minutes, until the tops are browned.
3. Garnish with the fresh herb and serve.

Crunchy Roasted Potatoes

Servings: 5

Cooking Time: 25 Minutes

Ingredients:

- 2 pounds Small (1- to 1½-inch-diameter) red, white, or purple potatoes
- 2 tablespoons Olive oil
- 2 teaspoons Table salt
- ¾ teaspoon Garlic powder
- ½ teaspoon Ground black pepper

Directions:

1. Preheat the toaster oven to 400°F.
2. Toss the potatoes, oil, salt, garlic powder, and pepper in a large bowl until the spuds are evenly and thoroughly coated.
3. When the machine is at temperature, pour the potatoes into the air fryer oven, spreading them into an even layer (although they may be stacked on top of each other). Air-fry for 25 minutes, tossing twice, until the potatoes are tender but crunchy.
4. Pour the contents of the air fryer oven into a serving bowl. Cool for 5 minutes before serving.

Crispy, Cheesy Leeks

Servings: 4
Cooking Time: 15 Minutes

Ingredients:
- 2 Medium leek(s), about 9 ounces each
- Olive oil spray
- ¼ cup Seasoned Italian-style dried bread crumbs (gluten-free, if a concern)
- ¼ cup (about ¾ ounce) Finely grated Parmesan cheese
- 2 tablespoons Olive oil

Directions:
1. Preheat the toaster oven to 350°F .
2. Trim off the root end of the leek(s) as well as the dark green top(s), leaving about a 5-inch usable section. Split the leek section(s) in half lengthwise. Set the leek halves cut side up on your work surface. Pull out and remove in one piece the semicircles that make up the inner structure of the leek, about halfway down. Set the removed "inside" next to the outer leek "shells" on your cutting board. Generously coat them all on all sides (particularly the "bottoms") with olive oil spray.
3. Set the leeks and their insides cut side up in the air fryer oven with as much air space between them as possible. Air-fry undisturbed for 12 minutes.
4. Meanwhile, mix the bread crumbs, cheese, and olive oil in a small bowl until well combined.
5. After 12 minutes in the air fryer oven, sprinkle this mixture inside the leek shells and on top of the leek insides. Increase the machine's temperature to 375°F (or 380°F or 390°F, if one of these is the closest setting). Air-fry undisturbed for 3 minutes, or until the topping is lightly browned.
6. Use a nonstick-safe spatula to transfer the leeks to a serving platter. Cool for a few minutes before serving warm.

Ratatouille

Servings: 4
Cooking Time: 60 Minutes

Ingredients:
- Oil spray (hand-pumped)
- 1 eggplant, peeled and diced into ½-inch chunks
- 2 tomatoes, diced
- 1 zucchini, diced
- 2 bell peppers (any color), diced
- ½ red onion, chopped
- ½ cup tomato paste
- 2 teaspoons minced garlic
- 1 teaspoon dried basil
- ¼ teaspoon sea salt
- ⅛ teaspoon freshly ground black pepper
- Pinch red pepper flakes
- ½ cup low-sodium vegetable broth

Directions:
1. Place the rack in position 1 and preheat oven to 350°F on CONVECTION BAKE for 5 minutes.
2. Lightly coat a 1½-quart casserole dish with oil spray.
3. In a large bowl, toss the eggplant, tomatoes, zucchini, bell peppers, onion, tomato paste, garlic, basil, salt, black pepper, and red pepper flakes until well combined.
4. Transfer the vegetable mixture to the casserole dish, pour in the vegetable broth, and cover tightly with foil or a lid.
5. Convection bake for 1 hour, stirring once at the halfway mark, until the vegetables are very tender. Serve.

Fried Corn On The Cob

Servings: 2

Cooking Time: 10 Minutes

Ingredients:

- 1½ tablespoons Regular or low-fat mayonnaise (not fat-free; gluten-free, if a concern)
- 1½ teaspoons Minced garlic
- ¼ teaspoon Table salt
- ¾ cup Plain panko bread crumbs (gluten-free, if a concern)
- 3 4-inch lengths husked and de-silked corn on the cob
- Vegetable oil spray

Directions:

1. Preheat the toaster oven to 400°F.
2. Stir the mayonnaise, garlic, and salt in a small bowl until well combined. Spread the panko on a dinner plate.
3. Brush the mayonnaise mixture over the kernels of a piece of corn on the cob. Set the corn in the bread crumbs, then roll, pressing gently, to coat it. Lightly coat with vegetable oil spray. Set it aside, then coat the remaining piece(s) of corn in the same way.
4. Set the coated corn on the cob in the air fryer oven with as much air space between the pieces as possible. Air-fry undisturbed for 10 minutes, or until brown and crisp along the coating.
5. Use kitchen tongs to gently transfer the pieces of corn to a wire rack. Cool for 5 minutes before serving.

Classic Baked Potatoes

Servings: 4
Cooking Time: 50 Minutes

Ingredients:
- 4 medium baking potatoes,
- scrubbed and pierced with a fork

Directions:
1. Preheat the toaster oven to 450° F.
2. BAKE the potatoes on the oven rack for 50 minutes, or until tender when pierced with a fork.

Roasted Eggplant Halves With Herbed Ricotta

Servings: 3

Cooking Time: 20 Minutes

Ingredients:

- 3 5- to 6-ounce small eggplants, stemmed
- Olive oil spray
- ¼ teaspoon Table salt
- ¼ teaspoon Ground black pepper
- ½ cup Regular or low-fat ricotta
- 1½ tablespoons Minced fresh basil leaves
- 1¼ teaspoons Minced fresh oregano leaves
- Honey

Directions:

1. Preheat the toaster oven to 325°F (or 330°F, if that's the closest setting).
2. Cut the eggplants in half lengthwise. Set them cut side up on your work surface. Using the tip of a paring knife, make a series of slits about three-quarters down into the flesh of each eggplant half; work at a 45-degree angle to the (former) stem across the vegetable and make the slits about ½ inch apart. Make a second set of equidistant slits at a 90-degree angle to the first slits, thus creating a crosshatch pattern in the vegetable.
3. Generously coat the cut sides of the eggplants with olive oil spray. Sprinkle the salt and pepper over the cut surfaces.
4. Set the eggplant halves cut side up in the air fryer oven with as much air space between them as possible. Air-fry undisturbed for 20 minutes, or until soft and golden.
5. Use kitchen tongs to gently transfer the eggplant halves to serving plates or a platter. Cool for 5 minutes.
6. Whisk the ricotta, basil, and oregano in a small bowl until well combined. Top the eggplant halves with this mixture. Drizzle the halves with honey to taste before serving warm.

Florentine Stuffed Tomatoes

Servings: 12
Cooking Time: 2 Minutes

Ingredients:

- 1 cup frozen spinach, thawed and squeezed dry
- ¼ cup toasted pine nuts
- ¼ cup grated mozzarella cheese
- ½ cup crumbled feta cheese
- ½ cup coarse fresh breadcrumbs
- 1 tablespoon olive oil
- salt and freshly ground black pepper
- 2 to 3 beefsteak tomatoes, halved horizontally and insides scooped out

Directions:

1. Combine the spinach, pine nuts, mozzarella and feta cheeses, breadcrumbs, olive oil, salt and freshly ground black pepper in a bowl. Spoon the mixture into the tomato halves. You should have enough filling for 2 to 3 tomatoes, depending on how big they are.
2. Preheat the toaster oven to 350°F.
3. Place three or four tomato halves (depending on whether you're using 2 or 3 tomatoes and how big they are) into the air fryer oven and air-fry for 12 minutes. The tomatoes should be soft but still manageable and the tops should be lightly browned. Repeat with second batch if necessary.
4. Let the tomatoes cool for just a minute or two before serving.

Roasted Root Vegetables With Cinnamon

Servings: 4

Cooking Time: 20 Minutes

Ingredients:

- 1 small sweet potato, cut into 1-inch pieces
- 2 carrots, cut into 1-inch pieces
- 2 parsnips, cut into 1-inch pieces
- 2 tablespoons brown sugar (dark or light)
- 1 tablespoon olive oil
- ¼ teaspoon ground cinnamon
- Oil spray (hand-pumped)
- Sea salt, for seasoning

Directions:

1. Preheat the toaster oven to 350°F on AIR FRY for 5 minutes.
2. In a large bowl, toss the sweet potato, carrots, parsnips, brown sugar, oil, and cinnamon until well mixed.
3. Place the air-fryer basket in the baking tray and generously spray the mesh with oil.
4. Spread the vegetables in the basket and air fry in position 2 for 20 minutes, shaking the basket after 10 minutes, until the vegetables are tender and lightly caramelized.
5. Season with salt and serve.

Fried Eggplant Slices

Servings: 3
Cooking Time: 12 Minutes

Ingredients:
- 1½ sleeves (about 60 saltines) Saltine crackers
- ¾ cup Cornstarch
- 2 Large egg(s), well beaten
- 1 medium (about ¾ pound) Eggplant, stemmed, peeled, and cut into ¼-inch-thick rounds
- Olive oil spray

Directions:
1. Preheat the toaster oven to 400°F. Also, position the rack in the center of the oven and heat the oven to 175°F.
2. Grind the saltines, in batches if necessary, in a food processor, pulsing the machine and rearranging the saltine pieces every few pulses. Or pulverize the saltines in a large, heavy zip-closed plastic bag with the bottom of a heavy saucepan. In either case, you want small bits of saltines, not just crumbs.
3. Set up and fill three shallow soup plates or small pie plates on your counter: one for the cornstarch, one for the beaten egg(s), and one for the pulverized saltines.
4. Set an eggplant slice in the cornstarch and turn it to coat on both sides. Use a brush to lightly remove any excess. Dip it into the beaten egg(s) and turn to coat both sides. Let any excess egg slip back into the rest, then set the slice in the saltines. Turn several times, pressing gently to coat both sides evenly but not heavily. Coat both sides of the slice with olive oil spray and set it aside. Continue dipping and coating the remaining slices.
5. Set one, two, or maybe three slices in the pan. There should be at least ½ inch between them for proper air flow. Air-fry undisturbed for 12 minutes, or until crisp and browned.
6. Use a nonstick-safe spatula to transfer the slice(s) to a large baking sheet. Slip it into the oven to keep the slices warm as you air-fry more batches, as needed, always transferring the slices to the baking sheet to stay warm.

Fried Green Tomatoes With Sriracha Mayo

Servings: 4
Cooking Time: 12 Minutes

Ingredients:

- 3 green tomatoes
- salt and freshly ground black pepper
- ⅓ cup all-purpose flour
- 2 eggs
- ½ cup buttermilk
- 1 cup panko breadcrumbs
- 1 cup cornmeal
- olive oil, in a spray bottle
- fresh thyme sprigs or chopped fresh chives
- Sriracha Mayo
- ½ cup mayonnaise
- 1 to 2 tablespoons sriracha hot sauce
- 1 tablespoon milk

Directions:

1. Cut the tomatoes in ¼-inch slices. Pat them dry with a clean kitchen towel and season generously with salt and pepper.

2. Set up a dredging station using three shallow dishes. Place the flour in the first shallow dish, whisk the eggs and buttermilk together in the second dish, and combine the panko breadcrumbs and cornmeal in the third dish.

3. Preheat the toaster oven to 400°F.

4. Dredge the tomato slices in flour to coat on all sides. Then dip them into the egg mixture and finally press them into the breadcrumbs to coat all sides of the tomato.

5. Spray or brush the air-fryer oven with olive oil. Transfer 3 to 4 tomato slices into the air fryer oven and spray the top with olive oil. Air-fry the tomatoes at 400°F for 8 minutes. Flip them over, spray the other side with oil and air-fry for an additional 4 minutes until golden brown.

6. While the tomatoes are cooking, make the sriracha mayo. Combine the mayonnaise, 1 tablespoon of the sriracha hot sauce and milk in a small bowl. Stir well until the mixture is smooth. Add more sriracha sauce to taste.

7. When the tomatoes are done, transfer them to a cooling rack or a platter lined with paper towels so the bottom does not get soggy. Before serving, carefully stack the all the tomatoes into air fryer oven and air-fry at 350°F for 1 to 2 minutes to heat them back up.

8. Serve the fried green tomatoes hot with the sriracha mayo on the side. Season one last time with salt and freshly ground black pepper and garnish with sprigs of fresh thyme or chopped fresh chives.

RECIPES INDEX

J

Jerk Chicken Drumsticks 52

Jerk Turkey Meatballs 47

K

Korean "fried" Chicken Wings 81

L

Lamb Burger With Feta And Olives 57

Loaded Potato Skins 85

M

Maple Balsamic Glazed Salmon 37

Meatloaf With Tangy Tomato Glaze 60

Middle Eastern Phyllo Rolls 83

Midnight Nutella® Banana Sandwich 77

N

Nice + Easy Baked Macaroni + Cheese 26

O

Oven-baked Barley 22

Oven-baked Couscous 23

P

Paleo Spiced Zucchini Bread 16

Parmesan Artichoke Pizza 32

Pea Soup 27

Pecan-topped Sole 45

Polenta Fries With Chili-lime Mayo 87

Q

Quick Pan Pizza 24

R

Ratatouille 96

Red Curry Flank Steak 63

Ribeye Steak With Blue Cheese Compound Butter 65

Roasted Eggplant Halves With Herbed Ricotta 99

Roasted Fish With Provençal Crumb Topping 42

Roasted Pepper Tilapia 44

Roasted Root Vegetables With Cinnamon 101

Romaine Wraps With Shrimp Filling 40

Rosemary Lentils 28

Rotisserie-style Chicken 53

S

Sea Scallops 43

Shrimp & Grits 39

Skirt Steak Fajitas 66

Slow Cooker Chicken Philly Cheesesteak Sandwich 21

Spicy Beef Fajitas 10

Steak With Herbed Butter 59

Stuffed Pork Chops 61

Sunny-side Up Eggs 9

Sweet Or Savory Baked Sweet Potatoes 91

W

Warm Chocolate Fudge Cakes 70

Western Omelet 15

Printed in Great Britain
by Amazon